MOTHER AND MURDERER

For
Jessica

Mother and Murderer

The Sad True Tale of Rebecca Smith

SALLY HENDRY

THE HOBNOB PRESS

First published in the United Kingdom in 2022

by The Hobnob Press
8 Lock Warehouse
Severn Road, Gloucester GL1 2GA
www.hobnobpress.co.uk

British Library Cataloguing in Publication Data
A catalogue record for this book is available from the British Library

ISBN 978-1-914407-34-5
Typeset in Adobe Garamond Pro 11/13 pt.
Typesetting and origination by John Chandler

Cover illustration:
'The Execution of Rebecca Smith at Devizes, 1849'. Small, framed oil painting of the execution of Rebecca Smith at Devizes in 1849, she is depicted with her back to us, standing on the platform with one man holding her and another putting the noose over her head.

CONTENTS

PREFACE

MARKET DAY in Devizes on Thursday 23 August 1849 was a day like no other. Usually the Market Place, with its elegant Georgian buildings and its plethora of coaching inns, would be bustling with hawkers, farmers, tradesmen anxious to sell wares, market stalls, cattle, sheep and horses.

But on this day the town was instead filled with empty carts and deserted carrier wagons; shops and inns were abandoned; for a far more interesting and tragic event was unfolding just a mile away.

Indeed, from early that morning, roads into the town from all directions had been jammed with carts and carriers, people riding and walking with some even taking to the waterway and packing a specially decorated canal pleasure boat from Pewsey Wharf. The *Wiltshire Independent* newspaper reported seeing mothers with babes in arms, small children held by their hands, and women dressed in silks with parasols to protect their complexions from the midsummer sun.

They had all come to see the public execution of 42-year-old Rebecca Smith, who had admitted to poisoning eight of her own babies. Her story had been reported avidly by newspapers across the country from London to John O'Groats and even came to the attention of the then Home Secretary Lord Grey.

She was to be the last woman in England to be hanged for infanticide of her own child. Following her death extenuating circumstances saved all 39 of the women convicted of infanticide between 1849 and 1864. But they could not save Rebecca. She had been convicted of the death by poisoning of Richard her eleventh child, but while in prison awaiting her execution she admitted to poisoning no fewer than seven of her other babies with rat poison stolen from hayricks. Some reports say she placed the poison on her breasts and fed her babies, others that she placed it inside their mouths with a finger.

Her crime shocked Victorian England but, had she been tried today, Rebecca Smith is likely to have been convicted of manslaughter on the grounds of diminished responsibility.

Her crime was the more shocking and puzzling as the court had heard she had been brought up by 'parents of industrious and irreproachable character' and had been 'instructed in her duty towards God and Man'.

~~~

So what happened? We need to unpick the strands of Rebecca's life if we can even begin to understand how she was able to murder not just one baby, but many. We need to examine the truth and the myths behind Rebecca's tragic story, starting at the beginning and journeying right through to her gruesome end on that hot August afternoon in 1849.

I

LIFE IN A WILTSHIRE VILLAGE

REBECCA'S STORY started in the Wiltshire village of Bratton, just ten miles from where her life ended on the scaffold.

Her home village, where she lived until the age of 40, lies under the escarpment of downland on the northern edge of Salisbury Plain – that vast area now owned by the Ministry of Defence and used as one of the country's largest military training areas. Access to the plain is now limited to a few days each year but in Rebecca's day it was open – crisscrossed with trackways, remote farmsteads and thousands of sheep grazing on open pastures and hillsides.

Bratton is tucked into the valley of the steep downland, which rises to more than 750 feet and is home to Wiltshire's oldest and best-known white horse hill figure as well as the Iron Age camp, Bratton Castle.

Today's visitors to the white horse can walk an old drove track up to the crest of adjacent Combe Hill and get a perfect bird's eye view of the village nestling in the valley below.

The road from Westbury to Lavington runs through the village at the foot of the downs and is known as Melbourne Street. On either side in Rebecca's day there would have been allotments, orchards and smallholdings, now replaced by housing.

In the early nineteenth century the village was composed of three tithings known as Melbourne, Bratton and Littlestoke. The latter lay around the church, so while it now seems remote from the village, it is likely that the church lay at the centre of a long vanished settlement. There are springs here too, known as Stoke Water and once used as a public watering place for livestock.

The old tithing of Bratton lay around the Court House, a timbered medieval building that still stands at the junction of Lower Road and Court Lane, while Melbourne or Millbourne can still be traced by the main road through the village.

The white horse chalk figure seen from the road between Westbury and Bratton

At the time of Rebecca's birth, Bratton was predominantly a rural community dependent on agriculture. In 1831 200 out of 300 families were occupied in farming and at one time the parish had at least 14 farms. Flocks of 1,000 sheep and more were still maintained on the downs with the annual sheep washing an important village event. The Stradbrook which runs through the village would be dammed and the sheep dipped under the water.

While sheep farming was important, farmers also grew corn, wheat, barley to produce malt for beer and ale, along with beans, peas, turnips, and fruit. Horses and oxen would have been used to plough the fields – the account books of the farming Whitaker family early in the nineteenth century lists 18 cart horses with names from Smiler and Diamond to Colonel and Duke. Dairy cows with names like Cherry and Myrtle are also listed along with pigs and oxen.

This fertile land won the admiration of journalist William Cobbett as his *Rural Rides* took him along the road from Westbury to Devizes in 1826. He spotted abundant crops of apples, pears and walnuts.

> The land here is very good…the turnips are very good all along here for several miles …this is indeed singularly fine and rich

land. The orchards are very fine, finely sheltered and the crops of apples and pears and walnuts very abundant.

Like many villages, Bratton had developed along the spring line, and the fast flowing Stradbrook once served at least four mills. Two thirds of the parish is on chalk downland to the south and the remainder on low-lying clay, divided from chalk by a strip of upper greensand. This belt of land was particularly good for market gardening with fruit and vegetables regularly sent from the village to Trowbridge market.

Cobbett mentioned abundant crops of apples – in fact in 1842 there were 40 small orchards, and while nearly all have disappeared under housing, the village still bears witness to that bit of its history. Just a short walk from where Rebecca lived, the village still has its own community orchard boasting a large variety of rare Wiltshire species, such as the Wiltshire Monster, Roundway Magnum Bonum and the Corsley Pippin.

At the time Rebecca was born in 1807, there were just over 1000 people living in the village. By 1841 this had dropped to just over 700, a reflection of the hardships being faced by lean times in agriculture. Many

Bratton showing the Stradbrook where sheep were dipped. In the distance are the steps cut into the bank and used by Baptists on their way to immersion and baptism.

left for the towns in search of alternative work, while others ventured further afield in their search for a new life – emigration from Wiltshire in the 1840s was not unusual, with families making new lives in Canada, Australia and New Zealand.

Bratton today is well worth a visit. It still has an impressive range of historic buildings, the oldest of which is the medieval church of St James. The present church could have been built on the site of a Saxon church as some of its carvings are Saxon or Norman. In 1400, the church was rebuilt in the Perpendicular style and had plastered walls and wall paintings.

Many tracks lead to the church, but it was not until 1832 that a road was built from the village. Today the church can be reached either via Church Road which leads from Stradbrook or from the west end of the village. A steep and picturesque flight of stone steps was installed by a Victorian vicar leading from the vicarage in Garston Lane to the church. These lead to the bottom of the combe where the stream runs through the valley, and then climb up to the churchyard. Local legend has it that no matter how many times you count the steps you never get the same number – though it is believed to be 208!

In the early nineteenth century, while most village residents were occupied in farming, some would have worked in the village's four mills – a corn mill and three textile mills. Rebecca's years in Bratton would also have seen the beginnings of one of Bratton's best-known industries – Reeves Ironworks. The company started out with blacksmith Thomas Pepler Reeves and his two sons Robert and John. A foundry was developed producing agricultural machinery such as corn-drills and ploughs. By the time Thomas Pepler Reeves died in 1849, the business, sited in the middle of the village on what is now the village green, had expanded to include a paint shop, saw-pit and other buildings.

The village had a pub – the White Horse Inn, near to where the Duke now stands. There were seasonal events too – horseracing on the downs above Bratton Castle and the annual Bratton Revels. Bratton Fair or Revels were held in July on the Monday or Tuesday following St Margaret's Day. It is believed the village church, now dedicated to St James, had an original dedication to St Margaret.

The Revels were evidently great entertainment, though members of the Baptist chapel were discouraged from attending, instead enjoying Sunday school outings up to the top of the white horse. According to William Whitaker, writing his diary in the late eighteenth century, such fairs including those at Westbury, Trowbridge and Edington seemed to be home to a wide variety of goods. In his diary he refers to buying figgy cakes, books, boot strings, pins, handkerchiefs, scissors, toys, a copy of Aristotle, ribbons, gingerbread, cakes, looking glasses and even a ballad and dying speech for a penny. These were sensational accounts of the dying speeches of criminals on the gallows along with the description of the crimes committed and the execution. Sadly such a pamphlet was produced following Rebecca's death – a broadsheet headlined 'The Trial, Sentence and sorrowful lamentation of Rebecca Smith'.

There was also the popular Westbury Hill Sheep Fair. This was held in September and attracted sheep, cattle and horses from all over the country and as far away as Ireland. Livestock was driven across Salisbury Plain on dust tracks and drove roads. As well as a popular venue for the buying and selling of stock, the Hill Fair boasted cheapjack stalls selling everything from crockery to pocketknives.

The roads to and from the village in Rebecca's day would have had tollgates – a gate or a bar that was swung open to allow people and traffic through once a fee had been paid. There were at least four tollgates in Bratton – one of the tollhouses can still be seen on the road leading to Westbury while others would have been situated in Lower Westbury Road, by the Court House on the road to Trowbridge and near the blacksmith's forge in Stradbrook. There was also a plethora of tracks and drove roads, used to drive animals to market or pasture.

A very important aspect of village life was the Baptist faith. Rebecca's family were members of the chapel, and the teachings there undoubtedly formed the foundation of Rebecca's own strong religious beliefs, later to be mentioned in newspapers and at her trial.

Nonconformity was strong in this area as in much of West Wiltshire, and one of Wiltshire's earliest and best examples of a Baptist chapel was built in Bratton in 1734. Its erection followed years of non-conformist meetings in venues such as individual homes or farm barns. As early as 1701 a house belonging to Bratton landowner William Whitaker was 'set apart and from henceforth intended to be used as a meeting house for the exercise of religious worship by Protestant dissenters'. Even before this, there had been a group of Baptists at nearby Erlestoke in the 1660s and there are also records of Bratton villagers walking the three miles to Westbury to worship there.

The Bratton Baptist chapel was built on a piece of land known as Brown's Berry. The building, of red brick with a high-pitched stone tile roof and stone facings had a burial ground at the rear. Even Nikolaus Pevsner paid tribute to its importance as a prime example of eighteenth-century non-conformist architecture, describing it as 'externally a gem'.

An intrinsic part of Baptist faith is the belief in adult baptism, and before the chapel had its own immersion pool people were baptised in the Stradbrook. The sluice gates and stream bed would have been cleared out prior to the ceremony, and steps were cut into the bank for people to descend into the water. Women would have had lead weights sewn into the hems of their gowns to prevent the material from riding up in the water, and thus preserving their modesty.

Nonconformity was strong in Bratton and the Baptist chapel built in 1734 is one of Wiltshire's earliest and best examples. Rebecca and her family were regular attenders.

The Baptist chapel was a vital hub for the community, attracting both the village's landowning families as well as farm workers. Among early deacons are the familiar names of Reeves and Whitaker, but also listed are villagers who were servants and employees. Regardless of status or birth, all members were considered brethren with all members given a vote and equality encouraged. However, as Dr Marjorie Reeves points out in her book *Sheep Bell and Ploughshare*, some hierarchy still existed as shown by records of pew rents. These list names such as Whitaker but one pew of seven seats at the back was labelled 'free sittings for old people'.

By 1837 membership had risen to 157 from just 20 in 1777 and the chapel was dominating many aspects of village life, providing a moral compass with such projects as the Band of Hope to encourage abstention from alcohol, through to the provision of a regular Treat – a chapel alternative to the supposedly riotous Bratton Revels. Records from the chapel Sunday school mention the purchase of handkerchiefs to be given as rewards for those who did not attend Bratton Revels.

Indeed, when Jeffrey Whitaker died in 1775, he even left funds for an annual sermon to save young people from the evils of Warminster fair along with funds 'to help the poor of Bratton and to provide instruction for poor Bratton children in reading and writing'.

The chapel helped with money and support too, with the chapel minute books showing reference to gifts of food and clothing.

But the Baptist faith was not confined just to attendance at the chapel – it pervaded all aspects of life. The private lives of the members often came under the scrutiny of the chapel, with criticisms ranging from illicit sex to drunkenness, violence and even necromancy. In an entry in the chapel minutes from February 1845, we read of one member being admonished after he consulted a fortune teller in a bid to recover stolen goods. Another entry records the appointment of two brethren to inquire into the case of a chapel member who had gone to the public house 'and engaged in a disgraceful quarrel'. That entry was followed just a week later with the said offender being received back into the chapel 'having reported to the church his deep sorrow for his sin'.

In January 1840, one member was excluded 'for persisting after admonition in pursuing a matrimonial connection inconsistent with scriptural directions' while another was excluded 'after many admonitions for the sin of drunkenness'. Chapel minutes record the baptism of several members of Rebecca's family so we must presume their lives were conducted according to the beliefs and guidelines laid down for a moral and upright life.

So this community was Rebecca's home until 1847. She was born in May 1807, the sixth child of yeoman farmer William Prior and his wife Sarah. Her birth was registered in the church records, where she is given the Biblical spelling of her name as Rebeckah. She had three sisters, Sarah, Elizabeth and Mary, and brothers Edward and William. The family was close-knit and supportive to Rebecca throughout her lifetime though, as we shall see later, at her trial one of her sisters was unhappily compelled by the Crown to give evidence against her. Later

Rebecca was one of six children born to William and Sarah Prior. Note the Biblical spelling of her name.

still, following the trial and sentence, family members signed a petition pleading for a stay of execution.

The family were long established in the village with parish records noting Priors, Pryers and Priers as far back as the early 1600s. The family were comparatively comfortable – the title of yeoman famer indicates a landowner. When Rebecca's father William died in 1830, he owned land in Bratton and Westbury and left farming stock and implements of husbandry, household goods and cash valued at around £300 – about £34,000 in today's money. William was evidently educated, signing his will at a time when many would just make their mark, and books are listed among the family possessions.

Rebecca, like her sisters and her mother, probably never learned to read and write. Educating girls was not deemed important though her brothers were both able to read and write – as evidenced by signatures on documents and wills.

At this time the only schools in the village were fee paying, such as that run by Jeffrey Whitaker in Lower Road for 'young gentlemen', or those attached to the Sunday schools at church or chapel. The opening of the village's first National School proved too late for Rebecca who would have been 13 when it opened in 1820 in a building still known today as the Oratory. Evidence at both her trial and at the inquest of her baby son in 1849, referred to her making her mark rather than signing her name. In the newspaper coverage of her trial, she was described as virtually illiterate – 'she could read but imperfectly and what she did read she was scarcely able to understand'.

Rebecca's family lived in Lower Road not far from the homes of the Whitaker family – the village's most important landowning family. Joshua Whitaker acted as executor for the will of Rebecca's father dated 28 January 1830 and was later to play an important role in Rebecca's life.

William died in August 1830 and his will was proved on 13 September. Its detail gives a glimpse into the life of the family. William left land and possessions to his wife – 'I give and bequeath to my said wife Sarah Pryor all my farming stock and implements of husbandry and all my household goods and furniture'. He also left Sarah a four-acre parcel of arable land off the Lower Westbury Road on the outskirts of Bratton. Known as Stock Mead Close, this land was only part of the 12 acres occupied by Sarah, who was listed as a market gardener in the 1841 census. The tithe map and apportionment of 1841 show Sarah leased other land too, including a paddock, orchard, and pasture in Lower Road.

William's will was significant in the way it planned for his family's future – especially for his daughters. It decreed that after his wife Sarah's death, money from the sale of her goods and possessions should be divided equally between the four daughters – the sons taking over the family land.

And Sarah's will, written in November 1841 throws even more light on the family's standard of living and the sort of upbringing Rebecca would have experienced. It mentions household goods, furniture, plate, linen, china, books, and liquor.

The terms of William's will and its implications would doubtless have been known in Bratton being a small close knit village. So when Rebecca married near neighbour Phillip Smith just months after her father's will was proved, there was suspicion that he may have married her knowing that she stood to inherit a considerable sum of money on the death of her mother. That suspicion was later mentioned at Rebecca's trial.

Rebecca's family were opposed to the marriage – Phillip being known as a drunkard. Nevertheless, Rebecca did marry him, and their first child was born exactly nine months after the marriage. One can only speculate as to whether this was a reason behind what turned out to be a brutal and destructive marriage.

The couple married on 5 May 1831, just two weeks short of Rebecca's 24th birthday and a year after her father William had died.

[No. 28] **Banns of Marriage between**

Philip Smith

and *Rebeckah Prior*

Both of this Parish

1st Time, Sunday, *April 10th* by *I Hooper*

2nd Time, Sunday, *April 17* by *W. ......*

3rd Time, Sunday, *April 24* by *I Hooper*

Rebecca's banns: The published banns for the wedding of Rebecca and Phillip. They wed at St James church in Bratton on May 5 1831.

The wedding took place at St James church – for although the families were members of the Baptist chapel, legislation was not passed until 1841 allowing marriages to be solemnised in chapel rather than church. Her brother Edward Prior was a witness to the wedding together with near neighbour Thomas Mead. Phillip, who was a farm labourer, came from another long-established Bratton family. In the year Rebecca was born there were births registered for no fewer than six Smith babies, and the 1841 census for Bratton shows more than 40 Smiths including another Philip Smith born in 1801 and a Rebecca Smith born in 1821.

St James church, Bratton, where Phillip and Rebecca were married in 1831.

Weddings at this time would have been held between 8am and noon. In rural areas, popular times to marry were often tied to the agricultural calendar and this may have happened in Rebecca's case. She and Phillip married on a Tuesday. Rebecca is unlikely to have worn a white bridal dress – this only became popular after the wedding of Queen Victoria to Prince Albert in 1840. Most people would have thought it an unnecessary luxury to wear a dress just once, so Rebecca is likely to have worn her best dress that could be reused or dyed.

The couple's first child Jane was registered in the records of St James church on February 8 1832. Interestingly, the baby is noted as born not christened. Rebecca in common with her mother and sisters was a regular attender of the village's Baptist chapel where she would have professed to a belief in adult baptism rather than infant baptisms carried out in the Anglican church.

Married life for Rebecca was probably tough. As an agricultural labourer Phillip would have faced a seasonal employment that paid little and led to regular periods without work. Wiltshire was a low-wages county and in Bratton, a rural community dominated by a few Baptist farming families, account books show a life of hard work and hard living for farm workers. We know for instance that between 1830 and 1845 the landowning Whitaker family paid their workers every four weeks, first deducting the cost of food purchased for personal use such as flour, barley, and potatoes.

It was later said at Rebecca's trial that Phillip had been cruel to her since the start of her marriage and that he scarcely ever provided for his family. He was known to be drunken and abusive. Rebecca survived her tragic situation through the love and support of her family – her sister later testified in court that she often helped her out with food and money.

Phillip, Rebecca, and Jane lived in a cottage in what is now Melbourne Street – the main street through the village. It is likely that they occupied part of a building known as Whites. This was a spacious Elizabethan farmhouse, with mullioned windows and a thatched roof. There was a pump in the garden behind. The house had belonged to John Whitaker but had been subdivided into cottages for farm workers. The building can be seen on an old postcard but is no longer there, having been demolished by the War Department which purchased it in 1952.

However the owner of a neighbouring cottage claims to sense Rebecca's presence in her house and speculates that she may have visited there as a refuge from her husband. Rebecca's spirit is said to be present when only women and children are there – understandable when one considers her tragic life.

Rebecca was at the centre of a close and supportive family. Her sisters, Mary Newman, Sarah Callaway and Elizabeth Taylor, lived within minutes of her. Her mother lived the other side of the village – just a short walk away.

The Baptist community was a mainstay of Rebecca's life. It was later said in court that she was 'god-fearing and industrious, attending Sunday services and praying morning and night…praying for her preservation through the night and returning thanks and praying for more mercies in the morning'.

While living at Bratton, Rebecca gave birth to no fewer than ten children including her first born, Jane, who was to be the family's sole survivor. Her second baby was taken ill and died of natural causes. The births were sometimes barely a year apart, for example baby Phillip was born on October 10 1837, dying three days later. A year to the day later, Rebecca gave birth to another son, also named Phillip, who died aged just eight days. Two of the babies died from natural causes while the others, as she later confessed, were poisoned by her. Rebecca is said to have used rat poison which she called 'Blue' and which she stole from hayricks in and around the village. Some newspapers, with tabloid-like sentiment, professed that she had smeared the poison onto her nipples and breastfed her babies. Other reports, including the court report, claim she placed it on her finger and inserted it into her babies' mouth. All her deceased babies were interred in the burial ground at the Bratton Baptist chapel.

Rebecca would have had little choice over the size of her family. Prevention of pregnancy was not really an option at this time though there were some methods of birth control. These mostly comprised the condom, at this time made of sheep gut and tied with a ribbon and considered principally as a means of preventing venereal disease. There was also coitus interruptus or complete abstention – all these methods were the responsibility and choice of the man.

Women's attempts to limit the growth of their family seems to have mostly depended on prolonging nursing. Lionel Weatherby in his nineteenth-century *A Young Wife's Own Book* reported that the poor were so convinced that lengthy breast-feeding prevented conception that many continued for more than two years.

Another obvious option available to women was the inducing of a miscarriage – a method frequently used. Herbal remedies were passed

This cottage in Bratton's Melbourne Street is believed to be where Rebecca started her married life. Then known as Whites, it was divided into cottages for farm labourers. It was demolished in the 1950s.

down from generation to generation. Books on cookery and herbal remedies often contained recipes to 'bring on a period'. In Culpepper's *The English Physician*, there were references to sea holly which 'procureth women's courses'. Other remedies referenced were pennyroyal, black hellebore, garden rue and white saxifrage. Most of these were common herbs and would have been known to rural women such as Rebecca.

J.P. Holmes in his *Popular Observations on Diseases Incident to Females*, noted in 1831 that old women advised the younger to employ 'pennyroyal and other herbs of a forcing nature'.

Abortion, which had been made a statutory offence in 1803, may anyway have been most unacceptable to Rebecca because of her religious beliefs and upbringing, though there was a common belief at this time that until the foetus quickened, it did not have a soul.

There was frequent condemnation of the use of abortifacients, with physicians warning that such use could lead to death of both mother and baby. Thomas Bull in *Hints to Mothers* in 1857 warned women that 'if strong purgative medicines were used to induce miscarriage, the result was almost inevitably death'.

However, the common occurrence of abortion was frequently mentioned in the medical press. One contributor to the *Cottage Physician* noted that 'the use of large doses of Epsom or Glauber's salts to procure abortion is known to be very common'.

There was no shortage of quacks and pseudo-doctors offering help to women who feared another pregnancy. While such advertisements were inevitably couched in seemingly innocuous terms, there was no doubt to the reader of their real purpose. These included such advertisements as Farrer's Pills or Velno's Vegetable Syrup which were supposed to cure 'suppression of the menses'.

Given Rebecca's almost continual childbearing – babies sometimes less than a year apart, it is unlikely she made use of any of the above methods, but she would doubtless have been aware of them.

Large families were the norm in the nineteenth century, particularly among the working classes for whom additions also meant helping hands to earn for the family. Sadly, the incidence of early infant death was also very common.

At the time when Rebecca's children died, child mortality was considerable, particularly among the poorer parts of society. This is undoubtedly a reason why the early death of her babies did not attract suspicion – it happened too often in large families.

In 1840 about a third of children died before the age of five. We know that child mortality in the Westbury area was 30 per cent. Several factors contributed to high mortality rates among poor children, including vitamin-deficient diets and a complete lack of sanitation. Records from these times show cause of death are as diverse as convulsions, diarrhoea, and sometimes atrophy – a polite term for starvation.

Another reason for infant deaths was the popularity of laudanum-based medications to soothe and quieten babies. At this time laudanum cost just a penny for an ounce and there was a plethora of proprietary brands of medicine aimed at soothing or quietening children. These contained opium, treacle and spices and were widely used. Infants dosed with these quack medicines became disinclined to eat and malnutrition could follow. Infants also fell victim to a range of diseases now virtually eradicated, such as smallpox, whooping cough, diphtheria and measles.

Literature from the Victorian era echoes the prevalence of early death. *The Old Curiosity Shop*, *Little Women*, *Oliver Twist* and *Jane Eyre* all feature desperately sad scenes of childhood death – it was an all-too-common theme in Victorian England.

But sometimes the death of babies and children was no accident. Infanticide was of great concern – even being raised in the House of Commons in the 1840s when one MP and doctor shocked his audience by claiming that infanticide, 'was going on to a frightful, to an enormous, a perfectly incredible extent.'

By the 1860s, the problem was believed to have reached crisis proportions and figured as one of the great plagues of society, alongside prostitution, drunkenness, and gambling. According to some experts, it was impossible to escape from the sight of dead infants' corpses, especially in London, for they were to be found everywhere from interiors to exteriors, from bedrooms to train compartments. In the four-year period from 1842 to 1846, more than half the number of inquests held nationwide were for cases of infanticide.

Rebecca was very ill after the births – illness doubtless compounded by her life of poverty and hardship. She also worked in the fields herself – a hard occupation which would have earned her just four shillings each week, less that that paid to teenage boys.

While there was help available to the destitute, there is no record of Rebecca and Phillip receiving help. As we have seen, minutes of the Baptist chapel often refer to assistance given to families within the community, but Rebecca's family is never mentioned. Likewise, the parish overseers who were responsible for provision of both out relief like food, clothing, and money, along with referral to the Westbury and Whorwellsdown Union workhouse, seem not have been involved in her sad case.

In the 1841 census Rebecca, Phillip and Jane were still living in Bratton. Jane is listed as aged nine and Phillip is listed as an agricultural labourer. Just three years later, their life changed irrevocably with the death of Rebecca's mother Sarah. Her will, which she had written in November 1841 after the death of her husband, was proved in June 1844. Appointing Joshua Whitaker as her executor, she asked him to sell everything – 'all my household goods and furniture, plate, linen, china, books and liquors; all my farming stock and implements of husbandry, monies and securities of moneys and my personal estate'.

Once debts and expenses for discharging the will and for her funeral had been settled, Sarah bequeathed the remainder, instructing Whitaker to 'pay one fourth part of the net proceeds of my said personal estate unto each of my four daughters, Mary Newman, Sarah Callaway, Elizabeth Taylor and Rebecca Smith, to and for her absolute use'.

| City or Borough of _Sunlett Bratton_ , | | | | | | Enumeration Schedule. |
| Parish or Township of _Wilbury_ | | | | | | 7 |

PLACE	HOUSES		NAMES of each Person who abode therein the preceding Night.	AGE and SEX		PROFESSION, TRADE, EMPLOYMENT, or of INDEPENDENT MEANS.	Where Born	
	Uninhabited or Building	Inhabited		Males	Females		Whether Born in same County	Whether Born in Scotland, Ireland, or Foreign Parts
Bratton			*Ann Chapman*		3		Y	
			Sarah do		1		Y	
		1	*Benjamin Collins*	35		*Ag Lab*	Y	
			Betty do		70			
			Martha Cook		12	*Servant*	Y	
		1	*Robert Reeves*	50		*Tailor*	Y	
			Mary do		40		Y	
			Mary do		20		Y	
			Jane Brigham		87		Y	
		1	*Robert Reeves*	30		*Carpenter*	Y	
			Jane do		30		Y	•
			Ellen do		8		Y	
			Thomas do	6			Y	
			Anna do		2		Y	
		1	*Ann Nash*		13	*Servant*	Y	
		1	*Philip Smith*	35		*Ag Lab*	Y	
			Rebecca Smith		31		Y	
			Jane do		9		Y	
		1	*James French*	40		*Ag Lab*	Y	
			Jane do		36		Y	
			James do	12			Y	
			Elizabeth do		10		Y	
			John do	8			Y	
			Mary do		6		Y	
			Jesse Tinley	14			Y	
TOTAL in Page	5	1		19	16	✓		•

The 1841 census lists Phillip and Rebecca Smith living in Bratton with nine year old Jane.

Ironically, the reference to absolute use would not have meant the money actually belonged to the four sisters. Until the Married Women's Property Act became law in 1882, any monies or properties were deemed to belong to the husband.

Once the will was proved, each sister was left £100 – a large amount of money at that time and equivalent to about £10,500 in today's money. It must have seemed a windfall to Rebecca's impoverished family.

Rebecca gave birth to another son, Edward, just four months after her mother died. He died within a month. His death was followed in 1846 by yet another son, Edward who lasted just three days.

By 1847, Phillip, Rebecca and Jane had moved from Bratton where they had lived all their lives. They moved to Westbury – only three miles away but representing a huge change for Rebecca who had been ensconced in a familiar and supportive society of friends and family all her life. The move would change everything.

2

THE MOVE TO WESTBURY

B Y THE time Rebecca and her family moved to Westbury, the town was in decline with high unemployment and a workhouse packed to capacity with desperate people who needed help just to survive.

But it hadn't always been like this. The town, which lies under the great chalk escarpment of Salisbury Plain, had been a thriving centre for cloth production and boasted its own ancient origins. The settlement was mentioned in the Domesday Book, where it was referred to as Westberie and Wesberie – from West-burgh. The burgh part usually refers to a fortified place in Saxon times and the 1086 survey noted a large royal manor and a church. The current medieval church of All Saints is believed to be built on the foundations of this earlier church, while a potential site for the capital manor is at the junction of Market Place and Maristow Street, where a Georgian building known as the Manor House may indicate the site of an earlier building.

Six mills, swineherds, beekeepers, and potters are also listed in the description of the settlement in the eleventh century. The presence of the mills acknowledges the area's many fast flowing watercourses and the numerous springs and wells that rise at the foot of the chalk escarpment. This abundance later led to the town's prosperity through cloth manufacture. Doubtless pigs would have thrived on the plentiful surrounding woodland while the abundance of clay in the valley would have suited the potters – until recently a large clay pit on the outskirts of the town provided the ingredients for the local cement factory.

The Romans had been here too and there is evidence of extensive Romano-British settlement at the Ham and at Wellhead. Roman remains found at the Ham came with the discovery of iron ore on the site in the mid-nineteenth century. The discovery of iron ore , which may have been an indicator of the reason for the early settlement, was uncovered when workers were cutting the town's railway line in the 1840s.

Westbury first had permission for a market in 1251. Archaeologists believe the layout of the current marketplace, now populated with eighteenth and nineteenth-century buildings, probably reflects the extent of this. By the mid-nineteenth century the once flourishing markets were in decline. The market on Wednesdays was confined to pigs only while two other fairs, at Lent and Whit Monday, were mainly for pedlar stalls. Larger fairs were held on Easter Monday and in September when business was done in cattle, horses, and cheese.

Westbury railways station with the iroworks behind.

Prior to the parliamentary reforms of the nineteenth century, Westbury was what was known as a pocket borough, because it was under the control – or in the pocket – of one or two people. It was then able to send two members to Parliament with voting limited to the occupiers of just 62 homes or burgages. These properties were usually owned by one person who then had the opportunity to control the voting or to sell the representation of the town to the highest bidder. For instance in 1822 there were 61 burgage tenements, 57 of which were controlled by Sir

Westbury Market Place: On the far left is the Lopes Arms where baby Richard's inquest was held. The shop on the right is where Rebecca purchased the arsenic used to poison her baby.

Mannaseh Masseh Lopes who had purchased the borough in 1810 from the Earl of Abingdon.

He gave one of the seats to his nephew Ralph Franco, son of his sister Esther. Interestingly this same Ralph Franco had married into another of Westbury's families. His wife was Elizabeth Matravers – a member of that Quaker Matravers family that made and lost their fortune in the town's cloth mills and after whom the town's senior school is still named.

Lopes has an interesting history which throws light on the rules of nineteenth-century power and politics. His family were Portuguese Jews who had made their fortune as sugar planters and slave owners in Jamaica. He first entered parliament as MP for New Romney in 1802 – but he had to convert to Christianity first. The law at this time banned members of the Jewish religion and many other nonconformists, such as Quakers, from being elected. But he was also known as a borough monger – purchasing parliamentary seats for cash.

In fact in 1819 Sir Manasseh was discovered to have bribed the voters in two separate constituencies at the previous year's general election. At Barnstaple he was alleged to have spent £3,000 on bribing the voters while, at Grampound in Cornwall, Lopes was convicted, fined £1,000 and jailed for two years for electoral corruption . His sentence was remitted in September 1820 and just two months later he went on to represent Westbury. Grampound was a notorious rotten borough and a byword for electoral corruption. Then just a village, it sent two members to parliament despite having only 42 voters – some boasted of receiving

The Lopes Arms: The Lopes Arms in the Market Place was Westbury's most important inn, used for everything from election dinners to auctions and inquests.

three hundred guineas for their vote. At this time, new industrial towns like Leeds and Manchester had no representation at all in parliament.

The Lopes family seat was in Maristow in Devon and that name is still reflected in Westbury. Lopes changed the name of then Silver Street to Maristow Street when he purchased the borough. The street is still so named today, and what was his manor house still stands at the entrance to the street from the marketplace.

He also made his mark on the town's leading hostelry, changing its name from the Abingdon Arms to the Lopes (or Lopez) Arms. The Lopes coat of arms hangs over the pub frontage. He also funded the construction of a new town hall in 1815. The building, which still stands in the Market Place, has the family crest in the stonework.

Lopes was not MP for long – he vacated his seat to allow Sir Robert Peel to take over and enter parliament in 1829. Peel had lost his seat at Oxford and the then government were anxious he should remain as a member.

With the way elections were conducted at this time, often those elected had not even set foot in the town. One famous example of this was Sir Robert himself, later to be Prime Minister and to be renowned as the founder of the police force and the agent for the repeal of the unpopular Corn Laws.

The town's early prosperity had been down to the manufacture of cloth with several mills built on the network of fast flowing streams that crisscross the town. As early as 1433 Westbury clothier William Gawen was trading as far away as Norfolk. In the sixteenth century the town's reputation for cloth manufacture had grown, with John Leland declaring 'The towne stondith moste by clothiers'. The trade continued to grow and by 1783 the town boasted 15 clothiers. Just five years later, it was said the town's annual clothing return was over £100,000.

The trade created riches for a number of families who went on to share their good fortune with the town in the form of bequests, educational and religious donations, and construction of community buildings. These included the Phipps, Matravers, Gaisford and Gibbs families – and later the Lavertons. For instance, Quaker and mill owner John Matravers in 1814 left money to found a school for boys and girls – the family is remembered in the name of the town's present senior school. And above the south door entrance into All Saints church, there is still a wooden painted board listing the bequests and legacies left to the townspeople. These range from money for blankets to paying for coats and even underwear for poor people. In 1772, for instance, John Gibbs left money to pay for 'six strong coats and waistcoats of an olive colour' for six poor men of Westbury. And as well as money for the establishment of a school, John Matravers also left £1,000, the interest on which was to be used annually for buying clothing for 200 old Westbury women.

Today the town's woollen heritage can be seen in the buildings such as Bitham Mill in Alfred Street and Angel Mill in Church Street which have been converted to housing. The fast-flowing streams are still evident too, many can be heard rushing below ground through the open gratings, for example in Church Street and Alfred Street. There are reminders too of the decline of the industry. In the woods at Wellhead there are traces of brick and stone and a mill race where a five storey mill once stood.

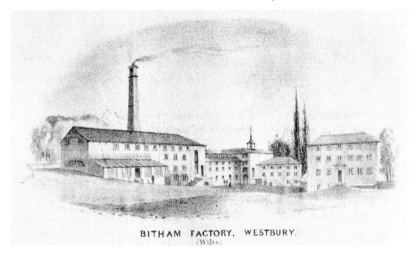

BITHAM FACTORY, WESTBURY.
(Wilts)

The once prosperous industry is also reflected in the town's wealth of historic buildings, including clothiers' houses such as those in Church Street and Westbury House – now the public library. There are signs too of past benevolence by community-conscious mill owners – the swimming baths in Church Street, the Laverton Hall in Bratton Road, Prospect Square, built to house millworkers, and numerous improvements to church and chapel.

But by the nineteenth century, things had begun to change. The introduction of mechanised production techniques created widespread poverty amongst both mill and agricultural workers, leading to poverty, civil unrest and in some cases even emigration in a bid to search for a better life.

The cloth industry was also prey to a number of adverse factors such as cheap imports and a falloff in demand. Westbury was already in decline when William Cobbett passed through in 1826 as he journeyed from Warminster to Devizes. The author of *Rural Rides* dubbed the town a miserable hole and described it as a 'nasty odious rotten borough, a really rotten place. It has cloth factories, and they seem ready to tumble down as well as many of the houses'. Much of his criticism was doubtless triggered by the town's reputation as a borough that could be bought and sold, but his criticism of its poverty is borne out by the signs of unemployment and distress in the early nineteenth century. By 1819, times were hard, with the unemployed set to digging for a paltry wage while their children were taught to knit stockings.

By the time Rebecca and her family moved to Westbury, the town was in the grip of an even worse economic crisis. Increased mechanisation combined with cheap lower-grade cloths from the mills of Northern England had affected orders and production leading to closures and layoffs, and in turn to unemployment and inevitable poverty. In July 1842, the *Wiltshire Independent* newspaper was reporting the' distressed state of the poor' in Westbury due to the temporary closure of the Matravers and Overbury mills, the town's principal employer.

Just months before Rebecca was hanged for her crimes, the local newspaper was advertising the sale of several mills owned by William Matravers. There was also an advertisement for the sale of his house and his furniture. He then lived in Westbury House, now the town's library. Just before this catastrophic slump in the cloth industry, there had been eight mills in the town. All were closed in the sharp downturn, and although the industry's fortunes revived in the 1850s, by the late 19th century there only two woollen mills left in the town – Angel and Bitham Mills.

These two mills were owned by Abraham Laverton, and later by his nephew William. Abraham, who had been born in a cottage in Trowbridge's Newtown, revived the industry when he purchased Angel Mill in 1851, going on to produce world-famous cloth that won medals at international shows. His obituary in the local newspapers referred to him as 'a self-made man' and his many business interests and investments accrued him a large fortune.

When Abraham died in 1886 at his Farleigh Castle home, he was a millionaire and one of the richest men in Wiltshire. He was renowned for his charitable donations in Westbury, funding schools, the Laverton Institute, funds for church and chapel, and a development of houses.

Now known as Prospect Square, these were built to house workers who had lost their jobs after voting for him in the elections. Prior to the introduction of the secret ballot in 1872, everyone's vote was public and open to corruption and bribery.

But in the 1840s prosperous times were far away. Admissions to the town's workhouse in Eden Vale more than doubled in just 12 months. In 1842 the workhouse was packed to its limit with almost 300 people and 30 others awaiting admission. The workhouse minute book of February 1850 notes the employment of an assistant porter for six weeks 'in consequence of the great number of able-bodied paupers in the House'. Analysis of the occupations of the inmates, as they were known, includes a wide range of workers from the woollen industry, from weavers to burlers.

The closure of the mills and the decline in agricultural work combined to create a perfect storm of poverty and need, with mill owners Phipps and Matravers telling a public meeting in Bath that even before the mill closures 'famine was already in the houses of the poor'.

A meeting of cloth manufacturers in the White Hart at Bath in 1842 was told that Westbury had 676 looms of which 354 were currently unemployed. One shopkeeper complained his takings were down by half. The pawnbroker whose shop was on the corner of Haynes Road and Bratton Road, was surviving on trade from the middle classes – the working classes had nothing left to pawn. Cottage rents had been dropped by 25 to 40%.

The parish made a valiant attempt to deal with the crisis – offering people made jobless through the mill closures the chance to repair local roads – but even that meant they would only be employed a limited number of days each week depending on the size of their family.

Inevitably the uncertainty of hard times bred considerable unrest. By 1839 there were 12 trade and benefit societies in the town along with a flourishing Working Men's Association. Growing attendance at Chartist meetings further reflected the concern of the working population.

Chartism was a movement for political reform and generated petitions to parliament containing millions of signatures. Among the reforms demanded were a vote for every man of 21 and over, a secret ballot at elections, and a fairer distribution of parliamentary seats dependent on population – we have already seen how tiny Westbury could elect two members while flourishing and heavily populated Leeds and Liverpool had no representation at all.

In 1839 more than 300 people attended a Chartist meeting held in Westbury marketplace, while another at Chalford saw crowds of up to 500. In April of the same year, a meeting of Chartists in the town proposed that every Chartist should have a gun hanging in his kitchen. That recommendation, although not actually agreed, made the newspapers all over the country.

The Chartist meetings must have been frightening events in the town, with newspapers reporting people being bludgeoned, stones being thrown, and weapons used. On 7 May 1839, town magistrates hearing that a Chartist meeting was to be held at Chalford, sent for a troop of the 10th Hussars from Frome and the Warminster troop of the Royal Wiltshire Yeomanry Cavalry along with special constables. At about half past seven, a large crowd passed through the town on their way to Chalford. Several leaders were arrested and sent to Fisherton Gaol to await their trial at the assizes. These were cordwainer William Tucker, labourer Harry Hopkins and spinner Thomas Reynolds.

The *Wiltshire Independent* newspaper reflected the establishment views of its property owning readership when it commented: 'It is to be hoped that the consignment of these notorious Chartist leaders will be the means of putting some check to that delusion which has been so widely spread, particularly in the manufacturing districts, and which indeed threatened to dissolve the very links of society'.

Incidentally, the Chartists had to wait a long time for results – the secret ballot was not agreed until 1872 and full male suffrage not until 1918.

Unrest was reflected in local politics too. Traditionally a Tory town, many leading voters switched their support away from serving MP Sir Ralph Lopes after he reneged in his promise to support reform. Leading names like Phipps and Matravers supported Liberal candidate John Ivatt Briscoe who scraped in against Lopes with just two votes in the 1837 election.

This then was the town that greeted the Smith family on their move from Bratton. By then the town had a population of around two and a half thousand and had a wide range of facilities and services. These included 13 inns, 9 bakers, and 11 boot and shoemakers – including one in Maristow Street making clogs and pattens. The 1841 census shows four butchers, no fewer than 22 grocery and general shops and three straw hat makers – a Mr Nash in the Warminster Road even made stays!

Inns like the White Lion, the Angel, the Lopes Arms, the Crown, and the Ludlow would all have been operating – their trade in ale augmented by the fact that they were the stopping off points for the many carrier and coach services travelling to Bath, Bradford, Frome, Trowbridge, Chippenham, Warminster, Salisbury, and London.

Travellers could also take a coach to Corsham, Bath or Chippenham, from where they could take the train to London; and Westbury was on the brink of another dramatic change with the opening in 1848 of the first railway line to the town.

This reflected changes across the country where communications were fast transforming the face of nineteenth-century life. Alongside the spread of the railways, the Electric Telegraph Company was set up in 1846 enabling instant information transfer – an invention that would have had a direct effect on knowledge and awareness. Thanks to the new technology, Rebecca's infamous trial and execution would horrify readers in drawing rooms and cottages from John o' Groats to London.

The development of the railway led to an unexpected boost in the Westbury economy. As we have seen, iron ore beds to the north of the town were discovered when the cutting for the railway line was made. Furnaces were built and by 1872, weekly production was about 400 tons and 200 men were employed. The business gradually declined, though received a boost during the First World War. It was eventually shut down in 1925.

The cutting of the railway line led to other discoveries too, ones that reminded everyone of the town's ancient origins. In November 1848, the *Illustrated London News* reported that labourers digging near the railway had unearthed a lead coffin complete with skeleton, two stone vases and an ornamental cup. Well known archaeologist William Cunnington excavated the site, discovering a plethora of Roman remains.

When the Smiths moved to Westbury, they farmed ten acres of land, doubtless with Rebecca's inheritance. It is very probable that the family lived in Lower Road, now Leigh Road. By the time of the 1851 census Rebecca was no longer alive and there is no trace of the family, but by looking at the names of neighbours mentioned in inquest and court reports as living very near her, it is possible to make an educated guess at her location. Elizabeth Cockle, a neighbour, lived there. Another friend, Jane Joyce, is listed there too. Both of these women testified at her trial in 1849 saying they lived very near her and had known her for two years, and at the 1851 census, two houses between their homes are marked as uninhabited.

The family's new home was on the very edge of Westbury. Lower Road, also known as the Lower Warminster Road, was then virtually rural, surrounded by fields and orchards with only a handful of houses skirting the road. Properties featured on early maps show substantial land attached so it would have been ideal for a family reliant on earning its living from the land.

From Lower Road it was almost a mile to walk to the town shops, chapel and church. But that walk into town would have taken Rebecca past the high walled and gated workhouse in Gooselands – now Eden Vale. She would have seen the inmates working in the allotments adjacent to the workhouse, or carrying water from the wells, or even the line of uniformed children as they took their weekly walk with the workhouse teacher. All of these sights would have been a salutary reminder of the consequences of hardship and destitution.

But hard times did come for Rebecca, and the family's new beginning soon turned sour. The money was squandered by Phillip. Rebecca was herself reduced to growing and selling vegetables in Trowbridge and working in the fields as a labourer – a tough job for a woman – and the four shillings each week that she earned was all the family survived on as her husband spent his money on alcohol. Her daughter Jane was later recorded as a needlewoman so may have taken in work to supplement the family income. The family also took in a lodger, Sarah Millard, to help add to the dwindling family funds. Ironically, this same lodger later testified against Rebecca.

Once the money was gone the family were back to poverty, but with one crucial difference: they were now living among strangers.

While Westbury is just three miles from Bratton, it was a different world. Rebecca had grown up in Bratton. The names of her Prior ancestors are in the church registers since the sixteenth century; her mother had lived nearby; her married sisters lived in the village and there were friends and relations she had known since her birth. In short, the people of Bratton knew her, respected her family and were aware of her circumstances. If they suspected her infants had not died from natural causes, they said nothing. In Westbury, however, her neighbours regarded her as a newcomer and were quick to express their suspicions when things went horribly wrong.

3
A BIRTH, A DEATH, ARREST
AND INQUEST

O N WEDNESDAY 16 May 1849 Rebecca gave birth to her eleventh child – a son which she called Richard. The birth was attended by midwife Jane Harris, of Westbury Leigh, who later had to call on the family several times to get the payment owed to her for her services.

She did not know Rebecca – it was the first time she had attended her. She later told the court Rebecca had been extremely ill in her confinement and was a sickly woman, but 'the child was a fine healthy child – a boy – a nice baby.' She stayed three hours after the birth, leaving Rebecca with her neighbours Elizabeth Cockle and Hannah Harris.

Elizabeth, whose later testimony helped to condemn Rebecca, was there at the birth, and popped in several times in the days following to help look after the baby. She noticed the baby had boils which she dressed.

Rebecca had told the midwife that she had lost nine children, telling her 'all my children do die when they are about one month old'. When the midwife called three days later, the baby was 'dressed very nice and by the side of the mother on the pillow' but Rebecca expressed concern saying the baby was fractious and crying. She continued to tell everyone the same – that the baby cried incessantly. Her lodger Sarah Millard later testified that she used to hear the baby crying 'a good deal' at night.

Neighbours tried to help. Jane Joyce who lived nearby often saw the baby and said it was a fine healthy boy. But when she called on June 11, she saw the baby was very white and ill, with Rebecca saying the baby could not eat or suck all night. Rebecca seemed very low in spirits and there was no food in the house.

Jane and her sister Hannah Bailey tried to help, mixing up cream of arrowroot to soothe the baby. A starch, arrowroot was often used in the

Victorian era, boiled with a little flavouring added, as an easily digestible food for children and people with dietary restrictions. Rebecca said the baby would not take it, but Jane took the baby on her lap and fed it. Richard was at first reluctant to eat, keeping his tongue to the roof of his mouth, but eventually took some sustenance. Jane noticed a running sore on the baby's head and dressed it with a lead-based ointment called unguentum that she had purchased from Taylor's chemist in the Market Place.

Newspaper advertisement for Taylor's chemist.

Elizabeth Cockle suggested syrup of rhubarb to help and suspected the baby was suffering from bile after he vomited something like the yolk of an egg. She told Rebecca to call for one of the two Westbury doctors, Mr Shorland and Mr Gibbs.

But although she told everyone the baby was ill, Rebecca refused to get medical help saying it would be of no use for such a young child – a statement that would help to condemn her in court.

Phillip Smith however did seek a doctor's advice. He returned to his home village and asked Bratton surgeon Henry Brittain for help. The doctor accordingly visited the mother and child, pronouncing the baby healthy. But he was much more concerned with Rebecca's condition, later telling the court: 'She was very weakly and knowing she had not proper sustenance I recommended her if possible, to obtain it'.

It is unlikely his recommendations were followed. With no money and no prospects, Rebecca and her new baby were faced with near starvation. Evidence was later given that there was no food in the house and that her sister frequently helped her out with gifts of food and money.

But despite being extremely ill, Rebecca made serious attempts to purchase poison, both before and after Richard was born. On 24 April she tried unsuccessfully to borrow mouse poison from a neighbour, and then nine days after the birth, when she was too weak to leave her house, she asked Caroline Mackey, the teenage daughter of a neighbour, to buy poison for her from Taylor's chemist in the Market Place. She gave her a penny and said the poison was needed to send to her sister in Bratton who was suffering from rats and mice. But Caroline was unsuccessful in her errand after her mother explained that two people were needed to buy poison.

Then when baby Richard was less than a month old, Rebecca, still weak from her confinement, walked into town. She was spotted by Prudence Mead, who had previously lived in Bratton, and who knew Rebecca. Prudence now lived in Duck Street just around the corner from the marketplace so it is likely Rebecca would have walked past her cottage as she made her way into town. Knowing she had lately given birth, Prudence asked her how she was, and Rebecca said she was very poorly and needed to sit down and rest.

Rebecca took up the offer of a rest in Prudence's house and told her she had come into town specifically to purchase poison to kill rats and mice, saying' she could not put anything out of her hands for them'. She stayed three quarters of an hour with Prudence, then asked her to accompany her to the chemist shop, knowing that a witness would be needed for purchasing poison.

Taylor and Co., later Chards, was a reputable chemist and wine merchants. Sandwiched between the White Lion and the Crown in the

Market Place, the building still stands today but now houses a veterinary practice. Advertisements of their wares offered everything from Burton Ales and London Stout to cigars, fancy tobaccos and even William Flooks' Pills. The shop also sold poison.

In the shop, Rebecca requested a pennyworth of poison and apprentice Albert Mumford asked her what kind she needed. She said she was not sure, so Albert took down the white arsenic and showed it to her, explaining what it was. She agreed that was what she needed, and he weighed out a drahm on a piece of paper then double wrapped the white powder in two layers of paper – white and then blue – and wrote Arsenic Poison in large letters on the outside. He warned her to be very careful and specially to keep it out of the way of children as it was deadly.

Chard's chemist shop: Chards chemist in Westbury Market Place was formerly Taylors where Rebecca purchased the arsenic that killed baby Richard.

Rebecca replied that he need not be afraid as she was not going to use it herself adding that the poison was for her sister Sarah Callaway at Bratton, who was suffering with rats and mice. Her conflicting versions for wanting the poison so urgently was later to be used in court to convict her.

Rebecca walked home with her purchase though after her arrest she told local policeman James Burgess that she had thrown the package of poison into the stream behind the Baptist chapel in Cheap Street, now West End.

Back at the family home, baby Richard remained well until that evening, when he was suddenly attacked by pain and vomiting. He continued in this distressed state until he died just five days later on 12 June.

Rebecca called on Elizabeth Cockle at six in the morning to tell her about Richard's death, and she came round to help prepare the baby for burial. She brought a cap to place on the baby's head, but when she was laying him out, Rebecca warned her not to turn him over as she feared something may come out of his mouth.

Rebecca reported the death to the local registrar George Shorland. After ascertaining that the baby had been seen by a doctor, Mr Shorland entered the cause of death as unknown. He later told the court that Rebecca made her mark on the certificate – an indication that she could not write. The baby was buried on 16 June in the graveyard at Bratton Baptist chapel – the resting place of Rebecca's other nine babies.

But a perfect storm of circumstance and suspicion was shortly to change Rebecca's life. After Richard's untimely death, suspicions were voiced. Neighbours mentioned that though Rebecca had breastfed her child she had never called him by name. They noted her desperate attempts to purchase poison, her sad history of the loss of her previous babies, and the fatal coincidence of Richard's death. Even the midwife who had delivered Richard mentioned the suspicions to Rebecca who was reported to have responded with a shocked 'They say I murdered my baby!?'

Rebecca was arrested. Just eight days after his burial, the body of her last baby would be exhumed from its grave leading to a catastrophic chain of events. Within three months Rebecca's life would be over, but her crime would have made headlines in newspapers across Britain.

By order of the coroner, the body of baby Richard was exhumed from the graveyard on Friday 22 June by Bratton chapel sexton Humphrey Newman who had made the baby's grave just days before.

In her later testimony at Rebecca's trial, Humphrey's wife Anne said she had not been acquainted with Rebecca for two years – presumably since the family left Bratton for Westbury. But she added before that she had known her well and gave the court an insider's view of the accused woman.

'She attended the chapel. I never knew her other than a well conducted, industrious woman. She was of a kind disposition for aught I know' she said.

Humphrey took the coffin to James Burgess, the constable and bailiff of Westbury. He in turn locked it away at the Lopes Arms in the Market Place and gave the key to Dr Shorland who was to conduct the post-mortem with fellow Westbury physician John Gibbs.

A busy town centre inn may seem a curiously strange choice for a post-mortem and inquest, but as a venue it was not unusual. Coroners' inquests could be held in a local public house, ale house, municipal building, or parish workhouse, but sometimes in the building where the death had actually occurred. The inquest usually took place within 48 hours of a death that appeared to be suspicious or unexplained, and the role of the inquest was to decide when, how and by what means the deceased person met his or her death.

The Lopes Arms was then the town's leading hostelry. Believed to be on the site of the sixteenth century inn The Saint George and the Dragon, the inn was a venue for all kinds of events from election dinners to bean shows, property auctions to turnpike contracts. It regularly sent carriages to Westbury station, and was a pickup point for transport to villages and towns. It also had extensive stabling. The Lopes was not the only public house used for inquests – newspaper reports show inquests at other inns including the Angel in Church Street.

The coroner presiding at the inquest into Richard's death was George Sylvester, who lived at Castle Villa in Castle Street Trowbridge. This is now the building housing the Sylvester and Mackett legal practice, established in the late nineteenth century by a descendant of George.

Throughout the nineteenth century the role of coroner was held almost exclusively by members of the legal or medical profession. The coroner and a jury of between 12 and 23 persons, usually men of substantial standing and householders, examined the body, heard witnesses, and then came to a verdict as to cause of death.

Born in 1788, George Sylvester trained at Guys and St Thomas's hospitals and became a member of the Royal College of Surgeons in 1810. He became assistant surgeon on the Royal Navy and was aboard the Lion when it took Java in 1811. He was awarded a medal for this – a medal that incidentally was sold at Bonhams in 2013 for more than £3,000.

He was a coroner for 34 years, retiring in 1872. Among his celebrated cases was the 1860 inquest into the death of Saville Kent, the three-year-old victim of the infamous Rode Hill Murder. The murder was popularised in *The Suspicions of Mr Whicher* by Kate Summerscale.

George Sylvester died in 1887 less than three months from his 100th birthday and was reputed at that time to be the oldest legal professional in the country.

For attendance at the inquest of Rebecca's baby Richard, he would have been paid £1 6s. 8d – a fee laid down by the Inquest Expenses Act of 1837. Any medical witnesses at an inquest were also paid. The 1836 Medical Witnesses Act had introduced payment of one guinea for medical practitioners giving evidence or two guineas if they had to conduct a post-mortem – there were three such medical experts at the inquest into Richard's death.

At the inquest, the baby was identified by Rebecca's neighbour Elizabeth Cockle who had helped lay out the baby for burial, identifying the bonnet she had given Rebecca to cover the baby's head. When giving evidence, she said she had been a frequent visitor to her neighbour and that Rebecca had never once said the house was infested with rats and mice.

A post-mortem was carried out by George Shorland and fellow Westbury physician John Gibbs. They found all the organs apart from the stomach were healthy but a series of tests on the baby's stomach contents produced metallic arsenic. A second opinion was sought, and the samples were sent to one of the top experts in the country – William Herapath at Bristol. The inquest was adjourned, and Rebecca was remanded into the custody of the local constable.

She told him that she had not understood the proceedings and did not feel she had the chance to speak, a charge he refuted.

William Herapath was a famous chemical analyst and the first person to detect arsenic in the body of a person who had been dead for more than a year. He gave evidence in many famous court cases involving poisoning and murder and was to give evidence at both the inquest and at Rebecca's trial. Prior to this time death by arsenic was very difficult to detect as many of the poisoning symptoms were similar to other diseases around at the time – only by post-mortem analysis could truth be revealed.

Herapath at this time was regarded by some as the most eminent chemical analyst in the country, but his career had started in a quite different direction. Born at the Pack Horse Inn in Bristol in 1796, he was at first expected to follow in his father's footsteps by becoming a maltster. But investigations into that trade gave him a passion for chemistry and changed the course of his career. He was one of the founders of the

Chemical Society of London and of the Bristol Medical School where he was Professor of Chemistry and Toxicology.

His interests were not confined to science though. He was a Whig politician at the time of the Great Reform Bill and was president of the Bristol Political Union, acting against the Bristol rioting of October 1831. He represented the ward of St James on Bristol council as well as being a justice of the peace and a senior magistrate.

As well as being celebrated for his appearances as expert witness at prominent poisoning trials, Herapath's chemical kudos made him a popular choice as endorser of products such as beer.

In 1856 for instance he passed a favourable verdict on Dent's Country Brewed Stout, declaring he had 'partaken of it for several days. I find it to be a nutritious beverage, well brewed and fermented and free from acidity and adulteration'.

In 1848 he was endorsing Jones's Patent Flour which could be used without yeast, and which the *Lancet* called 'one of the most valuable inventions of the age'. Herapath commented that the flour made a good and light loaf and would be ideal for use by troops.

And the year before his death in 1868, he was endorsing the products of Roger's Brewery in Bristol declaring its AK beer to be 'well hopped, bright and well brewed and consequently a wholesome and invigorating beverage'. One could suggest his skills might have welcomed him into CAMRA today!

Herapath suffered from diabetes and died at his Old Park home in Bristol in February 1868. He was 72 years old.

Herapath's eldest son William Bird Herapath also became celebrated – this time in the field of medicine. He trained at Kings College London, receiving honours in six specialisms including midwifery. He was one of the first to use chloroform and ether for childbirth – in June 1848, a birth announcement for his son noted that he had been 'safely delivered under controlled influence of ether and chloroform'. This was five years before Queen Victoria made chloroform the preferred choice of expectant mothers when she used it in giving birth to Prince Leopold.

William Bird Herapath died eight months after his father. He was just 48 and died of jaundice.

So one can see when William Herapath gave evidence at the inquest into baby Richard, he was a force to be reckoned with.

He confirmed to the coroner that Richard's death was due to arsenic, given by mouth more than once. As well as the arsenic, the post-mortem found milk and a small thyme leaf in the baby's stomach. Interestingly, thyme was frequently used in home medical remedies at this time. It was said to help with colic and stomach pain so maybe someone helped soothe Richard's painful end by spooning an infusion of thyme?

At the inquest in the Lopes the jury was sworn in and heard evidence from several people including Caroline Mackey, the young girl who had been asked to buy poison, and Albert Mumford, the apprentice that had sold the arsenic to Rebecca. Phillip Smith was called to appear and said the child was perfectly healthy when it was born, and that Rebecca used to nurse and feed the baby.

'I have been married 18 years to Rebecca Smith who has had by me 11 children born alive, the whole of whom excepting the eldest died in infancy. I was not aware that my wife had purchased arsenic, nor do I know what it was for,' he told the inquest.

He also stated that he had not benefitted financially from Richard's death. This statement may seem unusual but reflects the scandalous number of murders committed in order to reap the rewards of a financial pay-out from insurance clubs.

Concluding the inquest, George Sylvester asked Rebecca 'have you anything to state to the gentleman of the jury'. She replied 'No, Sir'. He then asked 'The witnesses who have given evidence are all present. If you wish to ask any of them questions, they can be brought up.' Rebecca again replied 'No'.

The jury then returned a verdict of wilful murder, but the proceedings were not over, as coroner George Sylvester called a second inquest – this time into the deaths of two of the other Smith babies. At this stage there were already suspicions that she had poisoned her other children – indeed some publications actually stated this as if it were fact. For instance, the *Lloyds Weekly Newspaper* of July 1 topped a page with the headline 'Supposed Murder of Eleven Children By Their Mother '.

George Sylvester also had his suspicions and ordered the exhumation and examination of the bodies of two of Rebecca's other children leading to a second inquest.

This exhumation took place at Bratton chapel burial ground and the remains of Sarah, who died aged 20 days in August 1841, and those of Edward who died on 29 June 1844 aged 15 days, were sent to William Herapath for examination.

In his journal, Herapath noted the receipt of 'a large square box on which the cover was sealed down with a crest similar to that of Mr

Shorland'. The box had three compartments containing the remains of the two babies plus a sample of soil tied up in a handkerchief. He found traces of arsenic in both the bodies and in the soil sample, telling the inquest:

'This is I believe the first incidence on record of arsenic being discovered after an interment of eight years and I therefore wish it to be circulated that the years have no effect on removing traces of arsenic'.

This was a significant finding which was to affect many subsequent investigations into poisoning. He also noted his belief that the arsenic had been administered to the children causing their death. 'It existed in too great a quantity to have been administered for medicinal purposes' he said.

This second inquest concluded that the two babies had died through arsenic poisoning but there was not enough evidence to determine who had administered it – so Rebecca's trial was to be held on just one count of wilful murder – that of Richard. Rebecca Smith left Westbury for the last time. She was taken to Devizes prison to await her trial at the town's Summer Assizes.

The newspapers reporting the inquest were certainly not sympathetic to the accused. They described her as 'a forbidding looking woman' and added that she 'maintained a most indifferent behaviour throughout the whole proceedings, and was removed from the jury room in custody, apparently far less excited than any of the parties that had been engaged in the inquiry.'

4

ARSENIC – THE POISONER'S CHOICE

REBECCA WAS not alone in her choice of arsenic as the most popular and convenient of murder weapons. The nineteenth century has become known as the arsenic century due to its prevalence not only as a deliberate and often accidental poison but also for its use in a wide variety of products from face cream to wallpaper, paint to fabric.

As the poison of choice for nineteenth-century murderers, arsenic was implicated in a third of cases involving the administering of a toxic substance. There were lots of reasons for its deadly popularity – it was unbelievably cheap and easily available from the local chemist simply by asserting the purchaser needed it to kill rats and mice. Half an ounce – enough to kill 50 people – cost just one penny: the same price then as a cup of tea. And while we have seen that Rebecca needed a witness with her before she was served in Taylor's chemist in Westbury, there were still many places where arsenic was readily available with no regulations.

A cartoon in *Punch* features this anomaly with an enthusiastic pharmacist only too pleased to hand over a pound worth of poison to a tiny girl barely tall enough to see over the counter. The little girl asks, 'Please mister will you be so good as to fill this bottle again with laudanum and let mother have another pound and a half of arsenic for the rats'. The obliging chemist responds with 'Certainly ma'am. Is there any other article'?

Another advantage of arsenic was that its use as a poison was exceedingly difficult

Punch cartoon: Punch reflected growing public concern with this cartoon showing the ease at which deadly arsenic could be purchased.

to detect. Especially if it was administered in small doses over time, the symptoms displayed by the victim were very often mistaken for those of common diseases like food poisoning, dysentery, and cholera. Until scientific advances in the mid-century enabled arsenic to be detected in a body, this poisoning method was almost foolproof. Scientist William Herapath, who testified at Rebecca's inquest and trial, was one such pioneer in detection.

Another reason for arsenic being favoured as a poison was that it had no taste or smell and could not be detected when easily mixed in with food or drink. When heated it was said to give off a smell like garlic. It looked innocuous enough too – a white powder that bore strong resemblance to flour or sugar.

Sadly, this frequently led to it being misidentified, and the nineteenth-century newspapers are full of shocking stories of accidental deaths when the deadly substance had been mistaken for flour and cooked into pies or puddings.

One grisly example occurred in Bristol in 1847 when a family of six died after a sister-in-law, lending a hand in the preparation of dinner, made a rhubarb crumble with what she thought was flour.

And the *Salisbury Journal* of May 21 1787 reported what was described as the hand of providential justice. A man had decided to poison his wife and children so bought a leg of mutton which he rubbed over with arsenic. He then told his wife he would not be home the next day but that she and the children should enjoy the mutton without him. She decided instead to make dumplings for tea and to save the meat till his return. When he returned home only to surprisingly find his family fit and well, he asked his wife to cook him some fish. However, shortly after eating them he was in agony. It turned out the fish had been cooked in the dripping from the mutton. He died two hours later after confessing his guilt.

One of the most well-known incidences of accidental poisoning happened in 1858 in Bradford, Yorkshire. And it was something as innocuous as peppermint humbugs that killed 20 people and left more than 200 people suffering the after effects of accidental ingestion of arsenic. The sweet seller in question, known as Humbug Billy, plied his trade with sweets made by his supplier who inadvertently added arsenic instead of sugar substitute after an assistant at the local pharmacy mistook the powders.

But in most cases involving arsenic, poisoning was deliberate. In the 1840s alone, there were almost 100 trials for criminal poisoning and the newspapers were crammed with reports. One motive for poisoning was undoubtedly the fear of starvation and the lack of money. Rebecca herself confessed that she feared her children 'would come to want' and may have chosen death to avoid them suffering a life of poverty and deprivation.

Sometimes though there were other reasons – the disposal of an unwanted spouse or family member who was perceived to be hindering the poisoner's life. Sometimes the poisoning had a monetary motive – there are many instances where the poisoner stood to gain from a pay-out from a burial club. Victorian England had a plethora of burial clubs – a kind of insurance policy where you would pay in a small amount weekly against the life of a family member and would in return be awarded a sum for burial costs if they should die. Some babies were insured in three or four burial clubs from birth. Death could result in a pay-out of several pounds.

In 1848, Mary May of Wickes near Harwich, was sent to trial charged with wilful murder – the poisoning of her brother with arsenic. The inquest heard that she had entered him into The New Mourners Society burial club in Harwich just two weeks before his death. A neighbour told the inquest that Mary May had counted on her brother's demise in order to get the £10 pay-out from the burial club and had planned to buy a horse and cart with it. Mary May had been married twice and had 16 children – all but one of them had died in suspicious circumstances.

In the same year, Mary Ann Geering was condemned to death at Lewes Assizes after being found guilty of poisoning her husband and two sons. All three had been enrolled into burial clubs which paid out on their deaths. Although she denied ever having arsenic, the court had heard from two separate Hastings chemists that she had purchased the deadly poison on at least seven occasions, ostensibly to poison rats. This highlights the ease at which arsenic could be obtained just by frequenting more than one shop. At this time there were no registers kept of purchases of the poison.

Sometimes the poisoning seemed almost casual – a heartless disposal of an inconvenience. One such example is reported in the *Taunton Courier* in January 1844. It covered the trial of two sisters who were convicted of poisoning their father with arsenic mixed into fish, gruel, and tea. The court then heard they wished to be rid of him because he would not let them go dancing!

For 32-year-old Bath woman Charlotte Harris, arsenic proved a way of ridding herself of her husband in order to wed her lover. Just three days after his funeral, she married 72-year-old William Harris who was conveyed to the church in a wheelchair. Charlotte, who sold oranges in Bath streets, lived with her husband stonemason Henry Marchant in Angel Terrace in Lower Bristol Road.

The inquest was held at the White Hart in Widcombe in May 1849 and Charlotte was committed for trial at the Somersetshire Assizes where she was found guilty of poisoning her husband by giving him gruel mixed with arsenic. The jury were unanimous in finding her guilty, but her defence lawyer pleaded for a stay of execution saying that Charlotte was pregnant – she had fainted several times during the trial.

The High Sheriff and officers then picked 12 women from the courtroom who were then sworn to try whether the prisoner was pregnant. The female jury retired for just a short time and confirmed she was indeed pregnant.

Presiding judge Mr Justice Cresswell, who was to try Rebecca's case in the Wiltshire Assizes just days later, then said the sentence of execution was respited and Charlotte, leaving court 'in a most pitiable state' escaped the gallows.

There was no such escape for 31-year-old Mary Ball for whom an abusive marriage combined with arsenic led to her hanging in 1849. She lived with husband Thomas in Nuneaton and had a violent stormy relationship; the husband having been known to beat his wife. The court heard Mary administered arsenic mixed in gruel for her husband's last deadly supper.

Arsenic was often also used as a means of suicide. The *Hampshire Chronicle* in 1838 related the tragic story of a mother who fearing destitution, mixed arsenic into a pudding, and ate it with her five children. They all died. One motive for poisoning was undoubtedly the fear of starvation and the lack of money.

Love, or the lack of it, sometimes became another sad reason for downing arsenic. A report in the *Warwickshire Advertiser* of October 1837 told of a 20-year-old woman who had taken arsenic because she had been neglected by her sweetheart. Dying, she had summoned the said man to her deathbed and begged him to follow her coffin to the burial ground.

The dreadful poison was also known to be used as a way of bringing on a miscarriage. An extraordinary story in the *Worcestershire Chronicle* of May 21 1839 relayed the tragic end of Ann Burton who died after taking arsenic to procure an abortion. She had been persuaded to take the poison by her live-in lover Joseph Leddington who gave her sixpence to buy it. He was charged with being an accessory to her murder. It was a tragic end to a strange life for Ann who had been sold with a halter round her neck at Stourport statute fair years earlier. Her husband had sold her to Leddington for half a crown, two shillings of which he threw back at Leddington, at the same time wishing him luck with his purchase! This episode reported in the newspaper, reflects the happenings in Thomas Hardy's book *The Mayor of Casterbridge* when a woman and child were sold at Weydon Priors (based on Weyhill fair near Andover).

Let us turn now to the actual effects of the poison – what did it feel like, how did it affect the body and the mind.

There is no doubt that ingesting arsenic was a terrible way to die that was neither quick nor painless. In a treatise on poisons written in 1817 it was described as a death that involved 'agonies that would soften the heart of a savage'. The effects usually started with a sensation of warmth or tightness in the windpipe – compared by victims to the pricking of needles. In 1842, at the trial of Mary Hunter her husband complained he felt as if 'he had swallowed cayenne pepper'. Another unfortunate victim said it was like having 'a ball of red fire' in his intestines.

The pain that followed was excruciating as the arsenic was taken into the blood stream. It caused vomiting and diarrhoea, pains in the muscles and bones and eventually heart failure. Evidence from witnesses in inquests and courts often refer to the victim having vomited a yellow substance. You will recall that Elizabeth Cockle had mentioned that baby Richard had vomited what looked like the yolk of an egg. And later, as she prepared the baby for burial, Rebecca had warned her not to turn the baby over for fear something may come out of his mouth.

Death could come in as little as two hours though some victims have been known to suffer as long as a fortnight before dying.

In order to evade suspicion, some poisoners would prefer not to administer one large dose but instead a series of smaller doses over a period of time. In this way the symptoms that ensued in the unfortunate victim were often similar to a gradual decline in health and might go undetected. Looking again at Rebecca's story, we can see that baby Richard took five days to die after her purchase of poison, and his reported symptoms manifested in crying, pain and vomiting, reflecting the gradual and deadly invasion of arsenic.

Whether eaten, inhaled, or absorbed through the skin, arsenic caused unimaginable suffering and relief often came only after three or four days, when a degeneration of the heart muscles finally brought about death.

But arsenic was not just the choice of would-be poisoners. It was the hidden killer immersed in a vast array of favourite Victorian products from wallpapers to toys, fabrics to cosmetics, paints to medicines.

It was used in a diverse range of industries from agriculture to manufacturing, even being used in fining white wines and in the making of cheap candles. Meat was dipped in arsenic to keep away flies, and it was used in farming as an ingredient in insecticides and fertiliser.

In August 1849, it was reported that a shooting party in Hampshire had been astonished at the sight of several dead partridges in the meadows. The birds were standing erect with their eyes open as if alive. Analysis of two of the birds showed they had consumed corn that had been treated with an arsenic compound.

Arsenic was also responsible for the deaths of a man and his two children after an old watering can, once used to mix wheat with arsenic in preparation for sowing, was inadvertently used to draw water from a well for cooking the greens for the family supper.

At the inquest that followed, concern was expressed that such a deadly poison should be left lying around and farmers were urged to take more care.

Back in the Victorian home, arsenic was prevalent in many products. Children's toys such as hobby horses, building blocks, dolls, crayons, chalks and watercolours were tainted with arsenical paint.

Paper given to children was arsenical and pupils were warned not to put the paper in their mouths. Shopkeepers covered their packages with arsenical paper and even used it on price tickets.

Even playing cards did not escape – analysis of a pack of green-backed cards by a Glasgow chemist detected more than a grain and a half of arsenic in each card – 83 to the deck.

One keen lady whist player with a penchant for green-backed cards even visited her physician complaining that after just a few hands of shuffling and dealing, her fingertips became so sore she could not play. Once she ditched the green cards, her fingers improved.

The green in question was an arsenical compound with titles such as Scheele's Green or Paris Green – and it was extremely popular as a colour for walls, fabrics, and even candles.

One of the most significant uses of the rich green colour was for fashionable ball dresses. As much as 20 or more yards of fabric could be used to make up a ballgown, and fashion dictated that deep green was the colour of the moment. However, analysis of a sample of green muslin by London practitioner George Rees found a square yard contained more than 60 grains of arsenical Scheele's Green. A contemporary cartoon in *Punch* entitled The Arsenic Waltz – the new Dance of Death featured well-dressed male and female skeletons preparing to dance – the lady inevitably wearing her arsenic infused ball gown.

THE ARSENIC WALTZ.

Dance of Death Punch cartoon: Popular periodical Punch gives its ironic interpretation of the popularity of Scheele's Green as a fashionable colour for ballgowns. The deep green dye contained arsenic and was eventually banned.

Wallpaper also contained the compound, even those fashionable designs produced by William Morris, who himself challenged what he called 'the arsenic scare'. However, he soon bowed to public opinion and changed the compounds used in dyes. In 1879, even Queen Victoria was affected by the green wallpaper scare. After analysis of a strip of palace wallpaper revealed arsenic, she ordered every bit of green wallpaper to be removed from the walls of Buckingham Palace.

So, we can see that arsenic was an intrinsic though deadly part of everyday life. One of the most surprising uses though was that of cosmetics and medicines. It was rumoured that the consumption of small amounts of arsenic boosted energy and metabolism. There were even claims that it increased virility and sexual power.

The supposition which created a craze for arsenic additions to everything from lotions to pills had started in 1851 when a Vienna medical journal had reported on peasants in southern Austria who ate arsenic regularly to increase strength and health.

A plethora of pseudo-scientific potions, soaps, wafers, and pills soon arrived on the market, many promising miracle results that endeared them to their hopeful purchasers.

Advertisements regularly appeared in the newspapers. One such example advertised Dr Mackenzie's Arsenical Soap. It promised 'a pearly skin and brilliant complexion'.

Similarly, Dr Campbell's Arsenic Complexion Wafers promised skin of 'unrivalled purity of texture, free from any spot or blemish'.

LADIES

If you desire a transparent, CLEAR, FRESH complexion, free from blotch, blemish, roughness, coarseness, redness, freckles, or pimples, use

DR. CAMPBELL'S
SAFE ARSENIC COMPLEXION WAFERS
—— AND ——
Fould's Medicated Arsenic Complexion Soap.

The only real true beautifiers in the world. *Warranted to give satisfaction* in every case or money refunded. Wafers by mail, $1; six large boxes, $5. Soap, per cake, 50 cents.

Address, H. B. FOULD, 214 Sixth Avenue, New York.
SOLD BY DRUGGISTS EVERYWHERE.

Ad for arsenic complexion: The addition of arsenic to cosmetics became popular in the nineteenth century. Products ranged from pills and soaps to face washes, all designed to make the skin fashionably pale.

Such advertisements were inevitably given an air of credibility by the frequent addition and endorsement of medical titles. In reality though, these products contained only the very smallest amounts of arsenic.

Arsenic was almost regarded as a sort of wonder drug with some of the most eminent figures in Victorian society believing that arsenic could be good for people. Some doctors even prescribed it as a cure for conditions including rheumatism, syphilis, worms, and morning sickness.

By the time Rebecca purchased her deadly poison, concern had already been voiced about the lack of regulations covering the purchase and use of arsenic. The rules were about to change.

In November 1847, the French government proposed restrictions on the sale of arsenic owing to the number of accidental deaths due to people mistaking the powder for flour, and from deliberate poisoning. It proposed that anyone with arsenic should mix it with Prussian Blue so there could be no mistake about it. The *Medical Journal* reporting on this said there were 20 to 30 deaths each year from arsenic being accidentally and innocently mixed with flour or other colourless food.

In 1848, there was a proposal that arsenic should only be bought with the signature of a licensed medical practitioner. Then in 1851, just two years after Rebecca was hanged for her crime, the government introduced The Sale of Arsenic Regulation Act. This tightened the often lax regulations around the sale of the deadly compound. It required sellers to have a written record of the purchaser complete with name, address, occupation, and reason for the proposed use of the arsenic. The buyer also had to sign the register.

There was also a requirement for a witness to be present at the sale. And there was a rule that arsenic should be mixed with indigo or soot to ensure it was never confused with such household items as sugar or flour. The legislation insisted on one ounce of soot for one pound of arsenic. For anyone failing to adhere to the new rules, there were penalties – they would be liable for a fine of up to twenty pounds.

5

IMPRISONED

FOLLOWING THE inquest and the committal to trial at the Assizes, Rebecca was taken to Devizes where she was held at the county gaol, also known as the New Prison, to await her trial. Rebecca may well have known Devizes. Just 13 miles from Westbury, it was a popular market town and was on the regular route for carriers from Westbury and Bratton. Simons' carrier van left the Crown in Westbury's marketplace every Thursday at 7am – doubtless for those wanting to make the most of Devizes weekly market.

Devizes lies almost exactly in the middle of the county and even boasted a brief spell as the county town, taking over from Wilton between 1655 to 1660. The town had grown in importance thanks to a Norman castle. Built in the eleventh century, the castle was known as *castrum ad divisas* – literally the castle at the boundaries. The castle was destroyed on the orders of Oliver Cromwell after Royalists, who had held the town in the English Civil War, surrendered to his Parliamentarian troops. Today the site is occupied by a Victorian Gothic castle.

John Leland visiting the town in the sixteenth century called it 'the town of Vies'. Then Cobbett in 1826 in his *Rural Rides*, referred to the town as a most famous corn market, and noted that 'Devizes is as nearly as possible in the centre of the county and the canal that passes close by it is the great channel through which the produce of the country is carried away'.

In its time the castle and the town played an important part in a struggle for the very throne of England between King Stephen and his cousin Matilda. The civil war eventually ended with an agreement that Matilda's son should become the next monarch and he succeeded to the throne as Henry II in 1154. Matilda left her mark though, granting the town freedom from some tolls and giving it the right to hold a market.

Anyone who knows the town today will be aware of the popularity

View of Devizes market place in the late 19th century.

of its markets which attract visitors from all over the county. One of the many buildings that pay tribute to its history is the Corn Exchange next to the celebrated Bear hotel in the Market Place. This was built by public subscription in 1857 after farmers and dealers had petitioned for a covered market to protect their produce. Topped with a statue of Ceres, Roman goddess of the harvest, the building was one of the largest public halls in the county. Its community role continues today – it was used as a COVID-19 vaccination centre in 2021.

By 1851 the town had more than six thousand residents. One of its appeals was its road network with some of its roads marked on early maps such as that of Ogilby in 1675. All the major roads were turnpiked in the early 1700s and by the mid-eighteenth century the town was approached by good roads on all sides.

The town was a main staging post on the road to Bath, and its many spacious inns and stabling are witness to this today. One of the most important inns was The Bear in the Market Place. By the late 1700s, 30 coaches daily were stopping there. The inn had its share of prestigious visitors including George III, Princess Victoria and Edward VII. The hostelry, which used to have ornamental grounds and a bowling alley, was the childhood home of famous artist Thomas Lawrence, who is said to have entertained such guests as David Garrick and Fanny Burney with his drawings and poetry recitals.

In 1810 the Kennet and Avon canal opened, linking Devizes with Bristol and London. The stretch through Devizes still contains the famous 29 locks, 17 of them in one flight at Caen Hill. The locks helped the canal rise 237 feet within two and a half miles. Cargo on the canal ranged from coal from Somerset to tobacco from Bristol, but fell into disuse in the late-nineteenth century. It was restored in the 1980s and the Caen Hill flight, opened by the Queen in 1990, quickly became a popular – though challenging – favourite with canal users.

The line of the canal took it past the front of the site where the gaol was eventually built – the very gaol where Rebecca was hanged in August 1849. On the day of her hanging, the canal proved its worth boasting one of the best views of the hanging. It was packed with craft, some specially commissioned for the occasion. Today, a bridge over the canal near the site is still called Prison Bridge – the only reminder of the building that once stood here.

The town's communication network was boosted with the arrival of the railway in 1857 though proposals for a railway service for Devizes had been made as early as 1836. The line eventually became a victim of the Beeching cuts and closed in 1966. At present there are moves to re-open a railway line to the town.

Devizes prison: Known as the New Prison, this was opened in 1817 and by the mid nineteenth century was the county's only prison. Described by William Cobbett as "a monstrous building", it initially housed 210 cells.

The importance of the town led to it hosting the annual summer assizes for Wiltshire following the Assizes Act of 1833. It was at these very assizes that Rebecca was to be tried – in the impressive classical style building that had been funded by local subscription. The court lay less than a mile from what became the county prison where Rebecca was to spend her last days.

The New Prison, or New Bridewell, had opened in 1817 to replace the town's Bridewell house of correction that had been used to contain prisoners since the sixteenth century. The former Bridewell became operational in 1579 after the opening of the Bridewell prison in London, so called because it was on the site of St Bridget's well and the old Bridewell palace of Henry VIII. The Devizes Bridewell, which is now a private residence in Bridewell Street, had 12 cells and six yards. When the prison reformer John Howard visited in 1774, he noted there were two night rooms and two day rooms, a yard, a workshop and an infirmary. The Bridewell eventually closed in 1836 and became the town's police station.

In 1835 Wiltshire still had four prisons: the Devizes Bridewell, the Marlborough Bridewell, Fisherton Anger county gaol and the New Prison at Devizes. By 1854, the latter had taken over as the county's only prison, taking prisoners from all over Wiltshire. The last to close was the county gaol at Fisherton Anger in Salisbury, which was about half the size of the Devizes institution. That prison had come under fire from inspectors for some time before its closure, with contrasts being drawn between discipline and management at the county's two large prisons.

At Fisherton there was no solitary confinement, no treadwheel, and prisoners had the luxury of all-day exercise 'from the time of being unlocked in the morning till a quarter before sunset in the evening'. Inmates could have visits up to three times each week, with friends and family bringing in food. The purpose-built Devizes prison, on the other hand, was a different story. It thrived on strict rules. Prisoners had to be silent, and a ban on communication was so extreme that the chaplain repeated his weekday prayers five times in separate wards so as to ensure prisoners in a larger group would not talk to each other.

There was work to be done too. Prisoners could be set to work for as long as nine and a half hours each day. The work was tough. Outside the prison walls, there was a treadmill that milled corn. Prisoners had to tread the wheel but were not allowed to speak to each other as they worked. Partitions separated each prisoner on the mill, and penalties were imposed for anyone who turned his head or looked over his shoulder. The treadmill provided work for 60 prisoners and an estimate in 1843 revealed that each man did the equivalent of a daily climb of 12,648 feet in under eight hours!

While this may seem barbaric, at least there was purpose to the treadmill – it ground the corn for the prison bakehouse. In some prisons however, the treadwheel had no other purpose than to punish prisoners! Introduced in 1818, the treadwheel was finally abolished in 1898 by the Prisons Act. Anyone who could not work at Devizes gaol was kept in solitary confinement. Those who rebelled against the draconian prison rules could face a dark cell without a bed and less food.

The difference between the town prisons was even more marked when inspectors assessed the cost of maintaining each prisoner. At Fisherton in 1839 the average daily cost per prisoner was one shilling and eight and a half pence while Devizes was just eleven and a half pence. There were other differences too. At Fisherton there was no education except by the chaplain who used the Bible as his textbook while at Devizes a schoolmaster was appointed in 1842 and each prisoner spent three hours each week learning reading and the church catechism.

The prison where Rebecca was to spend her last days was built just off the road to Bath, near the Kennet and Avon canal. There is no trace of where the prison once stood – housing now covers the site. The prison was officially closed in 1921 and demolished in 1927. Its demolition was filmed by Pathé News and the footage can still be seen on its website.

In its heyday the building would have dominated the Devizes skyline as travellers journeyed west towards Bath. William Cobbett, travelling through Devizes in 1826, gives us a first-hand view of the size of the prison saying: 'In quitting Devizes yesterday morning, I saw just on the outside of the town, a monstrous building, which I took to be a barrack'.

On being told that it was the prison, he commented that it seemed large enough to hold one half of all the able-bodied men in the county. In fact, the prison occupied almost 10,000 square yards of land enclosed by a 334 feet perimeter wall. The prison was designed by surveyor and architect Richard Ingleman who had submitted his design to a gaol committee in 1808. Initially it featured 210 cells, 16 exercise yards, two infirmaries and a chapel.

Built of brick and stone with convict labour, it encompassed all that was modern at that time, making best use of space and providing a sharp contrast to the old bridewells. It was a sixteen-sided polygon

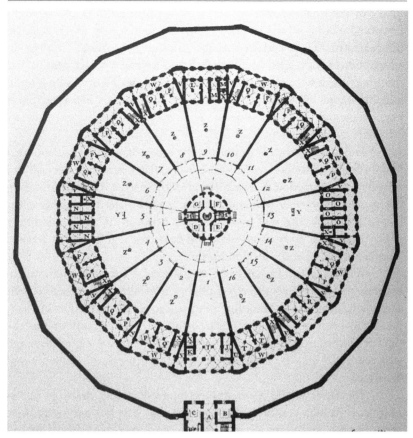

Devizes prison – diagram. The prison, built in the shape of a panopticon, contained everything from a bakehouse to a chapel, schoolroom, laundry and even a treadmill.

building, constructed on a plan of a panopticon, with the governor's offices in the centre tower surrounded by sixteen wards with exercise yards. The idea of the panopticon was coined by philosopher and social reformer Jeremy Bentham – the idea being quite literally seeing all – a design that made best use of space and enhanced efficient running of the prison as the governor was able to keep a close eye on the inmates from his central tower. Notes for the plans in 1808 declare 'the proximity to a circle imparts the strongest and most economical mode that can be devised for circumscribing the same extent of space'. The design was popular for institutional buildings and less than three decades later, the advent of the workhouse system under the New Poor Law saw many workhouses built on the same design.

By the time Rebecca was confined, the prison had added new cells for women along with a laundry room, bakehouse, day room, separate infirmary for sick prisoners, a chapel, and a schoolroom. In 1854 an advertisement for a schoolmaster offered a salary of £30 per annum – at the same time it was agreed that one of the turnkeys, Henry Rolfe, should have his annual salary increased from 40 to 50 guineas. Cells were 10 feet high, seven and a half feet wide and eight and a half feet long – women's cells were a little smaller.

The prison, which was built with convict labour, was surrounded by a 19-foot wall topped with loose stones to deter escapees. The wall had initially been topped with iron spikes, but these were removed following the escape of prisoner William Hunter in 1852 – he found the spikes helped him scale the wall and vanished, never to be caught despite a police search The prison was visited and inspected regularly with detailed reports published in the local newspaper.

While the prison had its own infirmaries for men and women, it seems that many people were suffering from illness even before their admission into prison. According to the surgeon's annual report in 1851, there had been 229 cases of illness of which 82 were suffering at the time of admission. He also notes that despite the prison being clean and well ventilated and drained, there had been outbreaks of influenza and diarrhoea.

The latter would seem unsurprising given that drainage up till 1857 was through cesspools. However, in that year not only were these replaced with sewage pipes at a cost of £130, but the prison also had pipes laid for gas and a new chapel was constructed. The following year the surgeon was noting that prisoners were in a healthy state much more than they would usually be at that time of year – he attributes this to the filling in of the cesspools and the fitting of new sewage pipes.

Reports of visiting inspectors in 1847 noted there were 163 inmates – 25 were female. Prisoners' behaviour was reported as 'attentive, orderly and becoming'.

The prison had its own chaplain, who was required to provide regular reports on the conduct, belief and behaviour of the inmates. During the time Rebecca was imprisoned, the chaplain was the Reverend Alexander Manning. A graduate of St Catharine's College in Cambridge in 1828, he had worked at Marlborough as chaplain to the Bridewell for seven years before taking up his post at Devizes in 1839 at a salary of £200 per annum.

Married with two sons Alexander and William, the chaplain lived in Long Street, Devizes – a select part of town where his neighbours included doctors, ministers, a professor of music and even a sculptor.

A compassionate man, he had his own views on the plight of the inmates he counselled. In 1847 he noted that the crimes that had led to their imprisonment were mostly minor and tellingly commented that many had been led to crime through need. 'Destitution and want are to many the causes of imprisonment, numerous commitments are of the inmates of the union workhouses', he stated in his chaplain's report.

But he was optimistic about the reforming nature of a spell in prison, saying that 'such is my opinion of the beneficial effects of their imprisonment in every respect that I cannot but feel confident that reformation has followed to a great extent'.

He often met discharged prisoners and their friends, eliciting favourable reports from them and spoke warmly of the prisoners' reverent attention during divine services.

But he was realistic about the role played by alcohol and drunkenness in the committal of crime. In another report to visiting inspectors in 1851 he gave his opinion that crimes such as burglary, highway robbery and sheep stealing 'are most frequently concocted in beer shops and public houses'.

Rebecca was the only condemned prisoner he dealt with during his time at Devizes. The next execution was in 1860 of a Spanish man Serafin Manzano who had been convicted of murdering Anastasia Trowbridge though he denied the crime. Having been brought up as a Roman Catholic Manzano was permitted to be visited by a priest of that persuasion, so the services of Reverend Manning were not required.

The Reverend's 28 year tenure at the prison was not without its difficulties. Shortly after Rebecca's execution, a disagreement between him and prison governor Thomas Haywood spilled over into civil court at the quarter sessions in Marlborough.

The governor accused him of 'general inattention and want of zeal in the performance of his duties'. He said the chaplain had been absent for three weeks without permission at the time Rebecca had been imprisoned awaiting her trial and that he had appointed a substitute chaplain without permission from the visiting justices who were responsible for overseeing the prison. He also said the chaplain had missed evening service on one Sunday, criticised him for giving too short a time for services and accused him of undertaking professional duties unconnected with the prison.

The chaplain argued that he believed he had been entitled to appoint a substitute just as he had on two previous occasions, and in answer to the charge about lack of zeal, he pointed out that he had missed evening service only once in ten years and that morning service always lasted between one and one and a quarter hours.

At the same hearing, which took place in the Ailesbury Arms hotel in the town's High Street, several charges of irregularity were also made against the prison governor. These included employing prisoners in a garden outside the prison walls and keeping dogs in the prison yard.

The chairman of the bench Sir John Awdry, who had also served on the jury that condemned Rebecca, acknowledged a degree of misunderstanding on the part of the chaplain but recommended that the rules of the prison should be strictly adhered to. He added that if Mr Manning should be obliged to leave home in the future, he would avoid a 'recurrence of this unpleasantness' by applying to the visiting justices first.

He urged the governor and chaplain to 'lay aside their unpleasant feelings towards each other, and unite their efforts for the public service'.

Mr Manning resigned his post through ill health in August 1867. He died the following year, leaving £200 in his will. His wife Sarah had died in 1864, and his oldest son in 1860 at the age of 27. Reporting on Mr Manning's death, the local newspaper described him as 'a man of considerable classical acquirements and of truly Christian heart'.

The Reverend's pertinent comments about crime being committed through poverty and need are borne out by committals to the prison in January 1843. Crimes then listed included stealing turnips, damaging a fir tree, refusing to work in the Devizes workhouse, and no fewer than 11 men and women charged with wilful damage and misconduct at the Melksham workhouse. One unfortunate inmate, Aaron Hughes, was whipped and imprisoned for one month just for stealing five silk handkerchiefs. Other frequent crimes over the decade were poaching, assault, vagrancy and leaving families chargeable to the parish.

From advertisements inviting supplies of goods for the prisons, it is possible to see that the prisoners would have been clothed in grey jackets, trousers and waistcoats. Other items included rice, best yellow soap, mop heads and brushes and oatmeal. Meat included chucks of beef and breasts of mutton; materials included yellow cloth, grey cloth, and yards of stout shirting. Bread was baked from the corn milled by the treadmill, and cooked in the prison bakehouse.

In 1861 the surgeon's quarterly report published in the *Devizes Gazette* noted that the prison was clean, well-drained, properly warmed, and ventilated. Ironically, when Rebecca was committed to the prison on July 7, it could well have marked an improvement in her living conditions. She would have had three meals daily, been given medical treatment and would have had someone to talk to her and pray with her.

Over the 31 days she was in prison, Rebecca was visited 39 times by the Reverend Manning and six times by a replacement chaplain. The rule was that, once a condemned prisoner was awaiting execution, he or she should be visited once per day – but that had been exceeded in Rebecca's case. The relationship between priest and prisoner must have been significant, for the very day after the trial where Rebecca had been convicted of murdering baby Richard, and while she waited in prison for the date of her execution, she made a startling confession to him.

She told him she had also murdered seven of her other babies – all had died within days of their birth. Two other babies had died from natural causes with only Jane, her first born, surviving of the 11. She said she had poisoned them using rat poison that she had found in the hayricks at Bratton. She called the poison 'Blue' and said she gave it to her babies on her finger (not as some more lurid newspaper reports would have it – that she breastfed the babies with the poison on her nipples).

This confession condemned her absolutely to the death sentence. When Home Secretary George Grey was considering two appeals for clemency for Rebecca, Judge Cresswell, who had presided at Rebecca's trial, wrote to remind him about her extraordinary confession. It literally condemned her – making it impossible for any leniency to be shown.

Looking back on the case in 1866 Sir George said: 'She poisoned her own child and there was great reason to believe she had poisoned several before. I suppose that was the reason which in the neighbourhood led to an absence of all sympathy for her and to the feeling that the punishment was not one that was uncalled for'.

6

THE TRIAL

REBECCA'S TRIAL took place at the Assize Court in Devizes on Thursday 9 August 1849.

The Assize Court, which was less than a mile from the prison, was near the banks of the Kennet and Avon canal, just a short walk from the town's marketplace. The building, which can still be seen in Northgate Street, near the Wadworth brewery, was constructed in 1835 and was funded by the people of Devizes, who were very anxious that the town should make its mark as one of the venues for the Western Circuit of the assizes, joining such cities as Winchester and Exeter.

The building was indeed impressive with its neo-classical lines reflecting its important status. Fronted by steps up to an entrance with four Ionic pillars, it housed two court rooms complete with balconies, along with offices and retiring rooms for judges and juries. The architect of this imposing looking courthouse was Thomas Henry Wyatt, who was also responsible for building the Wiltshire County Lunatic Asylum at Roundway near Devizes in 1849. T.H. Wyatt had a prolific and distinguished career and was elected President of the Royal Institute of British Architects. His reputation during his lifetime was largely as a safe establishment figure, well known for institutional architecture. His work in Wiltshire included the Romanesque church of St Mary and St Nicholas at Wilton, the town hall at Warminster, and restorations at All Saints church in Westbury where he worked on alterations to the west window in 1847.

Nikolaus Pevsner in his Buildings of England described the Devizes building as being designed while Wyatt was into Grecian or classical design, adding that it featured 'a dominant four column portico'.

At the time of writing, the building has been empty and quasi-derelict for several years, many aspiring redevelopment plans having failed. However, the latest plan for this important building is to become the home of the Wiltshire Archaeological and Natural History Society housing a museum with an array of world-famous collections relating to Devizes and its surroundings.

The judge at Rebecca's trial was Justice Sir Cresswell Cresswell. Born in 1794 to a family who could trace its heritage back to the 12th century, he had been educated at Charterhouse then Cambridge. Here he had the dubious wooden spoon honour of receiving the lowest place in the honours list of graduates. He nevertheless was awarded his MA in 1818 and was called to the Bar in 1819. He was a staunch Tory and supporter of Robert Peel and was MP for Liverpool between 1837 and 1842.

In 1858 he became the first divorce judge of the new Probate Divorce and Matrimonial Causes Act which created civil divorce – previously it had been dealt with in the ecclesiastical courts.

He was known later in life as a notoriously bad-tempered confirmed bachelor. He died in July 1863 after a fall from his horse, which had been startled by horses from a nearby broken carriage on Constitution Hill. He had no children and left all his £35,000 fortune to charity.

As the judge for the Western Circuit, he was obliged to travel around the West Country during July and August 1849. His timetable started at Winchester where he presided at the Assizes at the castle on July 10. This was followed by Dorchester, Exeter, Bodmin, Bridgwater and then Devizes where he arrived on Monday August 6.

Just days after passing sentence on Rebecca, his final stop on the judicial circuit was Bristol where it was reported he became very ill – his illness being of a 'choleric' nature. Today, choleric can mean bad tempered and irritable – and he may well have been – but the phrase in Victorian times related to illness of a bilious nature, possibly a disorder of the liver or gallbladder.

His arrival at Devizes in August 1849 was a cause for both celebration and ceremony. He arrived at four o clock, being met at a distance from the town by the Sheriff of Wiltshire Robert Nisbett and a full retinue. They escorted him to the court and then to his lodgings at what is now Handel House, an impressive early-nineteenth century three-storey building of Bath stone in Sidmouth Street.

At five o clock he attended a special service at St John's church and a sermon was delivered by the Sheriff's chaplain, the Reverend Francis Vansittart Thornton, from the 13th chapter of Romans verse 10, 'Love worketh no evil, for love is the fulfilling of the law'.

An engraving and a later photograph of the Assize Courts: Rebecca was tried at the Assize Courts in Devizes. The building was one of the venues for the Western Circuit Summer Assizes.

During the Assize week, a select party was invited to the Sheriff's residence, Southbroom House, to meet the judge. They were entertained 'in a style of great munificence'. The jury, who would normally have been entertained at the Bear, were also given the privilege of the High Sheriff's hospitality.

The business of the judiciary started at 10 o clock on the day after Justice Cresswell's arrival. The grand jury was sworn in and comprised: Sir F.D. Ashley, Bart., Sir John Whither Awdry, G.W. Heneage, R.B. Hale, S.W. Taylor, F.W. Rooke, G.E. Eyre, P.A. Lovell, J. Ravenhill, W. Browne, T. Smith, N. Goddard, J.B. Buller, J. Locke, Charles Phipps, T. Dewell, G.M. Esmeade, W. Coleman, Henry Gibbs Ludlow, C. Wyndham, W. Stancomb, and A. Awdry Esq.

At this time, all jurors were men. That would not change until 1919 when the Sex Disqualification (Removal) Act came into effect. The Juries Act of 1825 required jurors to possess property and be aged between 21 and 60. Jurors were generally gentlemen, merchants, professionals, wealthier shopkeepers, and artisans. Many held civic office such as being a magistrate.

It is possible to see this reflected in the jurors who tried Rebecca. Sir John Awdry, for instance, had been a judge in India, a fellow of Oriel College, Oxford and a JP in Wiltshire. He lived at Notton House, Lacock. Henry Gaisford Gibbs Ludlow was a magistrate and landowner, living at Heywood House near Westbury, while Charles Phipps, later to become Sheriff of Wiltshire, was one of the Phipps landowning family of Chalcot and Westbury. The last two would certainly have known Bratton and Westbury well and would have been aware of the tragic details of the case.

Unlike today, impartiality was not the rule. It was considered helpful if jurors knew the background to a trial or even the individuals involved. Given the extensive nationwide media coverage of Rebecca's sad story, and the reports of the inquests into her babies, it was unlikely that any of the jurors were ignorant of this case even before they stepped into the courtroom.

Indeed, some newspapers, including the *Lloyds Weekly London Newspaper* had virtually prejudged the trial, topping its reports of the inquest with the headline 'Supposed Murder of Eleven Children by Their Mother'. And this even before the case had come to court !

Rebecca would have been taken by closed carriage from the gaol less than a mile away for her appearance at the court. At the time the court was built there were underground cells for the holding of prisoners. The cells led along a dark brick tunnel to emerge in each court .

For this Assizes, there were 50 prisoners, but Judge Cresswell had informed the jury that the offences were generally of a light character – the case of Rebecca Smith being the only exception. He told the jury that with this exception, the cases they were to hear were straightforward and he congratulated them on the state of the county. In fact, cases that came before the court do seem trivial when measured against Rebecca's well publicised and shocking charge.

Maria Newman was accused of stealing some printed fabric and a shawl; James Price was convicted of burglary and theft, while aspiring parents Sarah and Thomas Dubber were acquitted even though it was shown they had altered the birth certificate of their son Thomas in order to make him eligible for a charitable apprenticeship scheme started by the Duchess of Somerset. Other cases before the court saw Phillip Wigmore and Christopher Trapp sentenced to six months imprisonment with hard labour for stealing clothes and absconding from the Warminster workhouse. The pair had optimistically tried selling the shoes, jackets and trousers clearly labelled Warminster Union Workhouse.

When Judge Cresswell moved to Rebecca's case, he reminded the jury that they would have two questions to consider during the trial: firstly, whether the baby died from poison; and secondly, whether the mother administered it.

Rebecca did have professional counsel – the Prisoners Counsel Act of 1836 had given prisoners the right to delegate the presentation of the defence. Prior to this, if prisoners wanted to put forward a defence, they could only do it for themselves – a task that was often beyond people who may have had scant education and a rudimentary ability to read.

The trial began at 9am when Rebecca was brought up into a very crowded courtroom. Mr Slade started the proceedings by summing up the case for the prosecution.

And he warned the jurors of their 'most solemn office'.

'You are here for the purpose of inquiring into the death of one fellow creature, and that on the result of that inquiry hangs the life or the death of another'.

Rebecca's indictment was read out before the court: 'For the wilful murder of her infant child, at Westbury, by administering to him a quantity of deadly poison, called white arsenic, on the 8th of June, and on other days between that day and the 12th of June on which day he died.'

The trial lasted from 9am to 5pm and 20 witnesses were called, starting with Rebecca's erstwhile neighbour Elizabeth Cockle, whose detailed testimony at the inquest had already effectively condemned Rebecca.

She said she lived near Rebecca and had known her for about a year. She described baby Richard as 'a fine child, full grown and presented a healthy appearance' and said she had seen the baby every day from its birth to its death. She had helped to lay out the baby and had identified him when the body was exhumed for the inquest.

Next up was neighbour Caroline Mackey who told the court that Rebecca had asked her to buy a pennyworth of poison so she could send it to her sister at Bratton to deal with rats and mice.

Then Prudence Mead who had noticed the ailing Rebecca in the marketplace, gave testimony, saying she accompanied her to the Taylors chemist where Rebecca bought a drahm of white arsenic to kill mice.

Other testimonies followed. Albert Mumford, the chemist's apprentice, spoke of selling the poison to Rebecca, and then midwife Jane Harris took the stand. She told the court Rebecca had been very ill during her confinement and that baby Richard had been 'a fine healthy baby, full grown and a very nice baby' but Rebecca had told her that all her babies had died before they were a month old. On later visits, Rebecca constantly asked her if the baby did 'worsty'.

After she heard of the baby's death, she called on Rebecca to ask for payment for attending the birth, telling her that people were saying she had murdered her baby.

'She said: 'They say I murdered my baby!' and went on to deny ever visiting the marketplace to buy poison.

Other witnesses included Sarah Millard, who had been a lodger in the Smith home, and neighbour Jane Joyce who testified that Rebecca had asked her for poison, and who had helped soothe baby Richard when he seemed distressed.

Sexton Humphrey Newman told the court how he had buried and later exhumed the baby's coffin at Bratton chapel burial ground, while his wife Ann under cross examination said she had known Rebecca as a frequent attender of the chapel.

'She was a well conducted, industrious woman, of a kind and quiet disposition', she told the court.

Evidence was given by local doctors, George Shorland, John Gibbs, and Henry Britton. The latter had been asked by Phillip to visit the baby which he did, considering it to be healthy.

But he told the court he had been concerned that Rebecca was sick and weakly and recommended she should have proper sustenance – food!

Eminent chemist William Herapath gave detailed scientific evidence from his analysis of the body of the exhumed baby, saying that arsenic had been administered over some days, leading to the child's death.

Surely the most tragic of all witnesses was the last to give evidence. It was Rebecca's sister Sarah Callaway who had been forced to appear for the prosecution to testify against her sister. She said she had suffered rats and mice at her Bratton home but that her husband had sorted it and that she had never asked Rebecca to buy poison for her. But her testimony shed light onto Rebecca's sad home life.

'I saw her the day after the birth, she was sick and weakly. I saw her again in about a week. The child appeared to be very ill, it cried and was fractious. She suckled it, she was careful to it and kind to it'.

Sara said she also knew Rebecca's husband Phillip saying: 'He was not always kind to her. She was very badly off, and I took her food and money.' She added that her sister was dropsical and badly off but was taking the best care of the baby that she could.

Following the various testimonies, and a short break, Mr Hadow addressed the court on behalf of Rebecca. He started by reminding the jury of the importance of their role, saying that his client's life hung in the balance. He said the case was one of 'great doubt, of mystery and perhaps of suspicion', and referred to the publicity already generated in the newspapers, and which might be seen to bias the case against Rebecca.

'Many rumours have gone abroad respecting the case and had probably reached their ears. The nature of the charge was such as to cause revulsion in the mind and to create prejudice against the accused'. He begged the jury not to allow their horror at the crime to extend to Rebecca nor to allow their judgment to be warped by prejudice.

His defence was that the evidence was entirely circumstantial – depending on a chain of isolated facts that did not come home to the prisoner at the bar. He said there was no proof it had been his client who had administered the poison, and that it might have been given inadvertently to the baby. He also reminded the jury that Rebecca, following the birth, had been destitute, sickly and ill. 'And what so likely that the babe, drawing its sustenance from an ailing mother, should ail too, and pine away and die?'

He pointed out that Rebecca had no motive for killing her baby, referring to the many publicised cases of parents who disposed of their children in order to cash in on burial clubs. 'In short there was no motive whatsoever; and if the prisoner had meditated such a crime, would she have gone about it as she did, openly and asking neighbours to buy poison for her, or to accompany her to the shop to buy it herself?'. He reminded the jury that Rebecca had been seen as a quiet, inoffensive person who had been a kind mother, and questioned how unlikely it was that such a person would commit such a crime as murdering their child. 'The brute beasts even did not destroy their young, and they could not suppose that any woman with a child at her breast, drawing its life from her, could harbour so cruel, so evil, an intent.'

Mr Hadow concluded his case by saying Rebecca was entitled to the doubts raised in the evidence and therefore ought to be acquitted.

Judge Cresswell then summed up reminding the jury that this was a case that would require all their vigilance, impartiality and judgment. He told them to disregard any rumours they may have heard and to come to a conclusion only on the evidence that had been presented. The jury retired for less than an hour to consider their verdict, returning to unanimously declare that they found Rebecca guilty, but recommending mercy that she might have time to repent.

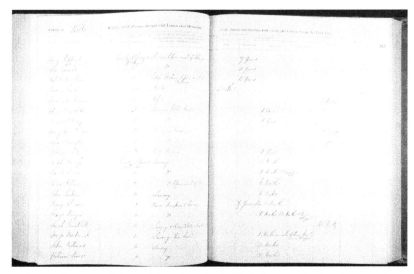

Criminal register: Rebecca is listed in the 1849 Assizes criminal register together with her sentence of death

But Judge Cresswell had no such compassion and was evidently convinced of Rebecca's guilt. Donning the nine-inch square piece of black silk, he gave a vociferous and damning tirade condemning her to the scaffold. He said he could not find the words to describe the horror of what she had done.

> Murder must under all circumstances ever be regarded as a most dreadful crime, but I want words to express my horror of it when it is perpetuated by a mother against her own offspring.
>
> There have been unhappy instances of the feelings of a mother being so overwhelmed with shame as to induce her to do away with her child in order to hide from the world the remembrance of a guilty intercourse. There have been instances where avarice has led to the same fatal result. But it has never before fallen to my lot to have to inquire into a case where the mother has been proved to have sacrificed her own child for no imaginable reason but to save herself the trouble of rearing it.

He said the jury's recommendation to mercy would be forwarded but said she should not hold out any hope at all. 'I should only mislead you and turn away your thoughts from repentance if I held out the slightest hope that your sentence will not be carried into effect'. He recommended Rebecca to the care and instruction of the prison chaplain saying: 'Remember that in a few days your life must go, and then you will commence an existence, for good or evil, to endure forever'.

He passed the sentence of death saying she should be taken from the court to the place of execution where she should be hanged by the neck until dead. Her body would afterwards be buried in the precincts of the prison. He ended by declaring 'May the Lord have mercy on your soul.'

Rebecca is said to have expressed no emotion on hearing the dreadful judgment. The *Wiltshire Independent* reported she seemed paler and more cast down than at the start of the trial. 'From the first she seemed without hope, and her general appearance was that of a woman to whom happiness had long been a stranger'.

Rebecca was led out of the court, through the tunnel and back to her cell at Devizes prison. The following day, she confessed to the prison chaplain Alexander Manning, admitting she had not only poisoned Richard but also seven of her other babies. She told him she had feared the children would come to want.

7

WHY?

LOOKING AT Rebecca Smith through the inverse lens of almost two centuries, it is a challenge to try and understand her actions and her crime. At the time, her tragedy merited both condemnation and sympathy.

To get as full a picture as possible it is necessary to look at the context of her married life, her economic frailty, her physical and mental wellbeing, her lack of legal rights and most significantly, her religious beliefs.

Looking first at the context of her married life, it is possible to see it was one of hardship, drudgery, and domestic abuse.

While Rebecca's family were established landowners, well respected and not short of money, she would likely have faced a radical change of lifestyle when she married just days before her 24th birthday. Phillip worked as a farm labourer like generations of Smith men before him. He would have been paid monthly and his pay would have been set against the bushels of flour, barley and potatoes provided by his employer. It is likely his take home pay was often under £1. Given that she came from farming stock and her mother was a market gardener it is likely that Rebecca would have grown or reared some of the family food. In her final years in Westbury, she raised money for food by growing vegetables which she sold at Trowbridge market.

When they lived in Bratton, Phillip might have earned extra money. The Whitaker family, which owned much of the land in the village, often offered extra tasks like harvest work, threshing, lambing, sheep dipping and shearing and turnip hoeing. There were also payments for rat and mole catching, with amounts worked out according to the number of tails produced.

The cottage they occupied in Bratton would have been tied to Phillip's work. This meant if he were to lose his employment, they could have been evicted. In the records of the Westbury and Whorwellsdown workhouse at this time, the census of inmates frequently features farm workers who had lost their home when they could no longer work. These include dairymaids, shepherds, farm labourers and blacksmiths.

But while Phillip had the opportunity to work and earn, it is likely the money was spent on drink at the local inn which was just up the road from their home. There are frequent references in court reports, inquest reports and newspapers, that Phillip was a drunkard, who failed to support his family.

Domestic abuse, then as now, is frequently hidden, so it is unclear whether Rebecca faced physical assault as well as neglect and deprivation from her husband. But her sister told the court that Phillip was not kind to his wife – and that may be a euphemism for domestic abuse. And when she was just hours from being executed, she expressed her great fear that Phillip would be cruel to 17-year-old Jane, her one surviving child.

Wife beating was commonplace at this time and only caused outrage if it was exceptionally brutal or endangered life. There was a widespread belief among ordinary people, male and female, that it was every man's 'right' to beat his wife so long as it was to 'correct her' if she did anything to annoy or upset him or refused to obey his orders.

And of course there was the infamous Judge Francis Buller, who in 1782 declared that a man had the right to beat his wife provided the stick used was no thicker than his thumb – a myth that found its way into common law.

In fact, the law weighed heavily on the side of the husband in nearly every way. When she married Phillip Smith, Rebecca would have given up any rights she had in common law and had entered into a contract that was virtually unbreakable. She would have promised as part of her vows before God to obey her husband. Everything she owned at the time of the marriage, or subsequently earned or inherited, belonged absolutely to her husband to dispose of however he pleased.

Her husband would have been seen as owning and having legal dominance over her, which sadly led to the belief that wives could be beaten. The law also allowed rape within marriage. The common law doctrine, known as coverture, allowed a married woman's identity to be subsumed in her husband's. Judge and politician William Blackstone, in his influential late-eighteenth century treatise on common law, states that 'by marriage the husband and wife are one person in law, that is the very being or legal existence of the woman is suspended during the marriage'.

JUDGE THUMB.
or — Patent Sticks for Family Correction; Warranted Lawful!

*Judge Buller The infamous Judge Buller was known for saying a man could beat his
wife provided the stick was no bigger than his thumb.*

Following on from that, married mothers at this time had no rights
over their children. All children born within a marriage belonged solely
to the husband, and the wife had no rights over them. If a couple parted

(even when the split was caused by the husband's bad behaviour) the father automatically had custody. Phillip could have prevented Rebecca from ever seeing her daughter Jane again.

So however terrible the marriage, leaving was not an option. Divorce was virtually unheard of and generally confined to the wealthy, as it necessitated the passage of a private act through Parliament. At this time there were only about ten divorces each year.

In short, Rebecca had no choices.

It is with this background, and at the insistence of Phillip, that the couple left Bratton for Westbury to farm 10 acres of land in Lower Road.

There is no doubt Rebecca's life was tough. Even after bearing ten children, she would still have worked all day in the fields before returning home to do all the household chores.

There would have been water to be carried, wood to be chopped before starting a fire for cooking or heating water, washing and other chores. Their lack of money would doubtless have led to a poor diet deficient in vitamins and insufficient to sustain a life of hard manual work. In her study of the Wiltshire farmworker, historian Avice Wilson refers to the very poorest of diets – breakfast being hot water poured over burnt crusts or over a little butter and flour.

We know women field labourers had a hard task, for often less than half of the wage earned by men, sometimes even less than that earned by boys. Barbara Haughton writing of life in a village near Pewsey in the mid-19th century said 'It is a hard life especially for the young girls and at a very early age the women look prematurely worn and haggard'. The writer was a daughter of a vicar in Pewsey but her descriptions in *In A Wiltshire Valley* reflected rural life across Wiltshire. She described rural farm workers being 'as laborious as they were ill paid. They had a hard struggle to support themselves and their families . . . their life was one unceasing struggle against an almost crushing poverty.'

A spotlight on the harsh life of a woman field labourer is also poignantly shown in Thomas Hardy's *Tess of the D'Urbervilles*, where he describes the relentless back-aching work, the harsh overseers, icy winds, the frost biting the fingers of the women as they toil in the fields.

Later in Victorian times the presence of women as field labourers declined for moral reasons – it was considered that young women were vulnerable both to male workers and the corruption of older women.

Given this background, it is unsurprising that Rebecca was far from well when she gave birth to her last child. Her midwife had said she was a sickly woman who was extremely ill after the birth of her baby as well as malnourished. The doctor who visited to look at the baby was more concerned about Rebecca, ordering her to get sustenance. Her neighbour Jane Joyce testified that Rebecca seemed 'very low' about her baby ailing, telling the court 'they were not very well to do . . . I saw nothing in the shape of food in the house.' Her sister told the court she often helped out with food for the family because they had none.

Rebecca might have been suffering from post-natal depression or at the very least shock and exhaustion – we can only guess. Some accounts suggest she may have been suffering from dropsy – the accumulation of fluid in the body such as the feet and legs – today known as oedema.

From the standpoint of the twenty-first century it is hard to know what Rebecca was really like – she leaves no diaries or journals, there are no portraits and her notoriety only came with her crime. She could not read or write. While Phillip signed his name on their marriage certificate, Rebecca made her mark. Registrar George Shorland recalled her making her mark on baby Richard's death certificate. It was said she barely understood the inquest or the court proceedings and did not take the opportunity to ask questions even when urged to do so. In fact, in their appeal for mercy, her family refer to her feeble mind.

But she was diligent and hardworking, and a loving mother to her firstborn child Jane. Her thoughts in her final hours were occupied by concern for her daughter's future and safety.

Sadly, there is no extant image of Rebecca save for a small oil painting of her execution, now in Devizes museum, but first-hand observations of her come from a variety of sources including neighbours, family members, fellow chapel-goers and of course newspapers. She was described as an inoffensive and industrious woman who was mild and contented in her deportment and free from guile or hypocrisy.

In their plea to the Home Secretary for the reduction of the death sentence, Rebecca's family stated that she had been brought up by industrious parents of irreproachable character, and that hopeless penury and domestic misery had led to 'the prostration of her feeble mind'.

One newspaper described her countenance as mild and somewhat benevolent, but when she was found guilty in court and sentenced, the same paper commented on her looking pale and cast down. She was later described tellingly as a woman to whom happiness had long been a stranger.

Another report said there was no doubt that she suffered great privations, her husband being given to drunkenness. It continued: 'We are more inclined to believe that some morbid propensity which under happier circumstances might have remained latent has been worked upon and developed by calamity sorrow and bitterness of heart till it produced the fearful fruits we have witnessed.'

Ann Newman, the wife of the Bratton chapel sexton, had known Rebecca from her years in the village. She described her as a well conducted industrious woman who was kind and quiet. She added that Rebecca frequently attended chapel.

The religious aspect of Rebecca's life is perhaps the hardest to take when trying to understand her crime, for how could she have reconciled the deliberate poisoning of her babies with the teachings of the Christian church?

There is no formal record of Rebecca in the minutes of Bratton chapel, though there are mentions of her mother and her sisters being baptised. However, several witness statements stress her religious beliefs, her attendance at services and her daily prayers. All her babies are buried in the Bratton chapel graveyard and it is unlikely that would have been permitted if she had not been a member of the chapel community.

Given that Rebecca lived the first 40 years of her life in Bratton it is unsurprising that she would have been heavily influenced by the chapel and its teachings.

The Bratton meeting house or chapel was, and still is, a prominent reminder of the important role of religion in village life. It was built in 1734 among the village orchards on a piece of land known as Brown's Berry, and by 1738 was holding two meetings on Sundays, a monthly church meeting, meetings of prayers and evening lectures on Sunday.

The chapel was extended in 1784 at a cost of £177 which was raised by the congregation, 15 of whom had also agreed to fund the salary of a minister – former Trowbridge clothier John Cooper. The membership of the chapel grew steadily in the early-nineteenth century and the chapel minutes diligently list the names of those accepted – and sometimes excluded – into the chapel community. The names include those we are familiar with throughout Rebecca's story such as Smith, Prior, Callaway Taylor and Newman.

Protestant nonconformity had been on the rise from the late seventeenth century. The 1851 census showed Wiltshire had 352 churches and 369 nonconformist places of worship, with Nonconformists numbering 45% of the population.

Nonconformity had great appeal, especially to the labouring classes. The more traditional and hierarchical Anglican church would be likely to have the lord of the manor or the labourers' employer seated in pride of place in their family pews, and services and ritual were archaic and formal. But the chapel or meeting house offered a welcome, less formalised worship and speech, and the opportunity for sharing thoughts and opinions. It also offered support, mutual respect, and benevolence. Bratton chapel minutes refer to help for needy families, support for children's schooling and the purchase of books.

Bratton historian and Oxford don Marjorie Reeves in her *Sheep Bell and Ploughshare* points out the community focus and extraordinary importance of the chapel in the lives of its members.

'The chapel community was one in which people of many different types, varying education and recognised differences of social standing found a common ground in religious experience and activity'. In fact, the chapel members ranged from the village landowners like the Whittaker family through to farm labourers.

When Rebecca appeared before the court, it was said she was very religious and that she attended the meeting house every Sunday and had prayers at home night and morning – 'praying for her preservation through the night and returning thanks and praying for more mercies in the morning'.

Given her life of dire poverty and facing a bleak future, she may have believed an early death was better than facing the sort of life she and Jane were going through. When she confessed her poisonings to the prison chaplain, she said she had feared the babies would come to want.

She may have felt the babies would be safe with Jesus rather than living a life of hardship and possible cruelty. Her religious beliefs may have made her think that new-borns, being free from sin and incapable of making moral choices, were innocents who would go to heaven.

For example, in Matthew 19 v. 14 Jesus said, 'suffer the little children to come unto me and forbid them not: for to such belongeth the kingdom of God'. And again, in Matthew 18 vv. 3-6 Jesus said Except ye be converted and become as little children, ye shall not enter the kingdom of heaven. In 1 Corinthians 7 v. 14, it is said a child is sanctified by the belief of its parents, so Rebecca may have felt her religious beliefs would assure her babies a place in heaven.

Nevertheless, it is exceedingly difficult to reconcile this with the fact that Rebecca caused her babies to suffer terribly before death. Death by poison is agonising and it is known, for instance, that baby Richard took days to die in considerable pain and distress. Many cases of infanticide in the nineteenth century refer to overlaying or suffocating – a gentler death.

Newspaper reports offered a range of possible reasons for her conduct with one ironically suggesting the deaths were a form of birth control.

But there may have been other reasons why Rebecca carried out these horrific crimes. For instance, by the time Rebecca conceived her last child, Jane was virtually an adult and may have been planning to leave home. Perhaps Rebecca would then have had the courage to leave as well. Another baby would have tied Rebecca to her desperately sad marriage for life.

Modern day examinations of motive for infanticide and child murder have come up with a variety of reasons. Research by psychiatrist Susan Friedman suggests there are typically five motives which might drive a parent to kill their child. The most common is a result of maltreatment or chronic abuse. Others include altruistic killing, when the parent is mentally ill or believes the child may be suffering. Another motive is seen in murders just after the birth of an unwanted child. Psychosis is another motivator, while the Medea complex, while very rare, is another. This is named after the Greek myth of Medea who is said to have murdered her children in revenge against her unfaithful husband Jason – she also killed his prospective bride!

While it is not always possible or useful to assimilate today's theories with historic events, it is tempting to attribute Rebecca's killings as altruistic, committed in the belief her babies would be better off dead, and thus sparing them a life of suffering.

Then again, the Medea complex is a possibility. Perhaps her actions were a bizarre way of striking out at the husband who evidently disempowered, repressed and reduced her to a wretched life of penury. At least two of the early babies were named after their father, and it is clear Phillip wanted a son. Indeed it was he who sought medical help when baby Richard was ailing. Perhaps in a marriage where she was completely disempowered, her actions were her only way of taking some control of her life.

Mental illness could also be a reason and it is necessary to examine

Rebecca's state of mind and consider whether she was mentally ill and incapable of understanding her actions and their consequences. She did however plan the poisoning in some detail, certainly of her last child Richard, so it would be difficult to suggest her actions were spontaneous or committed while in the throes of postpartum depression or psychosis.

Examination of infanticide both in the nineteenth century and more modern times, show that the act was often followed by the death of the mother by suicide. Rebecca is unlikely to have killed herself as the teachings of the Bible condemned such actions. But the very fact that she made no efforts to hide her many attempts to obtain poison to the extent of involving several neighbours, might in itself be construed as a suicidal act and begs the question – did she want to be found out and atone for her actions?

Certainly, were she to be tried today, it is unlikely she would be convicted of murder or manslaughter. Far more likely would be a call for a mental health review and a declaration by her defence lawyer that she was unfit to stand. While Rebecca's state of mind was not alluded to or offered as a defence at her trial, the Infanticide Acts of 1922 and 1938 abolished the death penalty for a woman who deliberately killed her newborn child while the balance of her mind was disturbed as a result of giving birth.

8

THE HANGING

Rebecca's tragic life ended on the scaffold at 12 noon on Thursday 23 August 1849. She was hanged in public at Devizes prison on a special platform erected on the top of the lodge at the main entrance to the prison. She was the fifteenth person executed in the UK that year, and she would be the last woman in British history to be put to death for the infanticide of her own child.

At this time in England all executions were held in public, and that would not change for another 20 years. Sadly, such events were a source of popular entertainment for Victorian England, often attracting thousands of spectators. The travel agency Thomas Cook even ran excursions to public hangings, treating them as tourist attractions. Spectators would gather hours in advance, sometimes the night before the event, jostling for the best places, paying for them if houses or rooftops nearby afforded a good view.

Such scenes frequently attracted fights – and proved a useful opportunity for pickpockets. Broadsides were frequently on sale at the place of execution. These were cheap printed sheets that provided a garish account of the murder, along with a crude woodcut illustration of the hanging. Sometimes songs were included, and there were instances where murderers went on to be portrayed as waxworks in Madame Tussauds or even as Staffordshire pottery figurines. Most notorious hangings sometimes made plays or puppet shows.

Moby Dick author Herbert Melville recorded in his diary paying half a crown for stand on a roof of a house adjoining the scaffold where husband and wife murderers Maria and Frederick Manning were hanged in 1849 in London. Other famous writers who witnessed public hangings and then made use of the memory in their novels include Thomas Hardy, whose witnessing of a hanging at the age of nine, led to him penning the sorry end of Tess in *Tess of the D'Urbervilles*. Charles Dickens also attended the execution of the Mannings and was 'astounded and appalled' by the scene. He later penned a letter of protest to *The Times*, appealing to Home Secretary George Grey to end what he described as a moral evil. His lengthy description of the event at Horsemonger Lane gaol, gives us an insider's view of the event and is well worth quoting.

> I believe that a sight so inconceivably awful as the wickedness and levity of the immense crowd collected at that execution could be imagined by no man and could be presented in no heathen land under the sun.

He went on to describe the cries and howls of the crowd, fightings, faintings, whistling and brutal jokes. There was even singing, with Mrs Manning's name being substituted for Susannah in the popular song.

'When the sun rose brightly – as it did – it gilded thousands upon thousands of upturned faces, so inexpressibly odious in their brutal mirth and callousness.' Dickens was not alone in voicing his horror – there was growing opposition – not to capital punishment *per se* but against the public aspect of the hangings. Campaigners said hangings should be conducted away from public gaze in the interior of the prison.

But that would not come to pass until 1868 when the Capital Punishment Amendment Act followed a two-year-long Royal Commission. Home Secretary Sir George Grey was among prison chaplains, gaol governors, prison reformers, lawyers and police providing evidence to the commission, which was chaired by Charles Gordon-Lennox, Duke of Richmond.

An appeal by five members for the abolition of capital punishment was turned down with one proposer sadly admitting 'I doubt that public opinion in this country is yet ripe for the acceptance of such a change'. There was opposition to Rebecca's execution in Devizes too. We have already heard that the jury in her case asked for her life to be spared in order to give her time to repent and consider her crimes. But there were two other appeals for

Sir George Grey.

clemency – commuting her sentence to transportation rather than death – and both were turned down by the Home Secretary Sir George Grey.

One of the petitions was signed by hundreds of Devizes people. But this petition, while it recommended her sentence be reduced to transportation, was not so much focused on Rebecca as on the concern around a public hanging and its effect on the town.

> We admit that there are no extenuating circumstances in this case pointing out the wretched criminal as an object for especial clemency, but our reasons for asking for a commutation of her punishment to transportation or imprisonment for life, are based firstly on the ground that public executions are useless as examples, tending to harden and demoralise the people, being invariably attended by drunkenness, debauchery and the commission of crime; and secondly that the unhappy woman may have time to repent.

The petitioners went on to note that the last execution in Devizes was in 1838 and the disgusting scenes at that event were still fresh in the minds of townspeople. The missive, with an addendum of several pages of tightly packed signatures, concluded: 'We hope this town may be spared the contamination which another such spectacle is sure to cause'. It added that far more signatures would have been added from townspeople had there been more time. The petition was headed and signed by John James Fox. He was a leading Quaker, a draper in business in the town, and a member of the Board of Guardians for the Devizes workhouse, as well as being one of the Commissioners for improving the town. A notice in the *Devizes and Wiltshire Gazette* in April 1840 mentions the annual meeting of the Commissioners at which one of their responsibilities in the town was 'removing and preventing nuisances and annoyances therein'. We can safely assume this would include the riotous behaviour and crime committed at public executions.

John Fox would have been a leading figure of influence in the town and had even bizarrely been elected as a churchwarden at St John's church despite being a Quaker. Following a public outcry he prudently backed out of the election! He lived with his family in St John's Street where he had a showroom regularly stocked with choice fabrics purchased from London.

On the document passed to Sir George Grey, it notes 'This Petition prays that the life of the prisoner might be spared on account of the demoralising effect of public executions.'

John Fox was not daunted by Lord Grey's refusal to act. Just a week after Rebecca's death, his impassioned plea for an end to capital punishment was printed in the *Wiltshire Independent*.

He refuted the idea that public executions acted as a deterrent, saying 'It must be admitted by everybody that to witness the hanging of human beings hardens and debases the spectators.' He went on to urge that government should be petitioned and 'the subject may be agitated till death punishments shall be swept from the statute book'.

We can see the Devizes petition had a much wider remit encompassing not just the safety of the town but also the whole issue of capital punishment *per se*.

The second petition sent to Lord Grey was the opposite – it was personal and especially sad and poignant. It was a heartfelt plea from her family and gave their view of Rebecca and the reasons for her crime. It is worth reporting in full:

> To the Queen's most excellent Majesty
>
> The humble petition of the undersigned relatives of Rebecca Smith now under sentence of death in the County Gaol of Devizes Most humbly sheweth:
>
> That while your Petitioners are unable to extenuate the fearful crime of which their unhappy relative has been found guilty by a Jury of her country, they are encouraged by a recommendation of that Jury to approach your Majesty and to implore a merciful consideration of her punishment.
>
> That the unhappy woman was brought up by parents of industrious and irreproachable character and instructed in her duty both toward God and Man and they can only attribute absence of all right feeling evinced by her awful crime to the prostration of her feeble mind by hopeless penury and the despair arising from domestic misery.
>
> That your Petitioners although they cannot but look for most severe punishment as the just consequence of the crime, yet venture to hope that commutation of the sentence of death may be graciously extended, and the wretched criminal allowed time to awaken from a state of mind to which sin and misery have brought her, and to seek mercy and forgiveness from Almighty God.

RECEIVED
H.O
AUG 18
1849

8853

To the Queen's most excellent Majesty.

The humble Petition of the undersigned relatives of Rebecca Smith now under sentence of death in the County Gaol of Devizes Most humbly sheweth.

That while your Petitioners are unable to extenuate the fearful crime of which their unhappy relative has been found guilty by a Jury of her Country, they are encouraged by a recommendation of that Jury to approach your Majesty, and to implore a merciful consideration of her punishment.

That the unhappy woman was brought up by parents of industrious and irreproachable character, and instructed in her duty both towards God and Man, and they can only attribute the absence of all right feeling evinced by her awful crime, to the prostration of her feeble mind by hopeless penury and the despair arising from domestic misery. That your Petitioners although they cannot but look for most severe punishment as the just consequence of the crime, yet venture to hope that a commutation of the sentence of death may be graciously extended, and the wretched criminal allowed time to awake from a state of mind to which sin and misery have brought her, and to seek mercy and forgiveness from Almighty God.

Your Petitioners most earnestly implore your Majesty, that the sentence of death passed on the said Rebecca Smith, may be commuted to such other punishment as your Majesty in your wisdom and mercy may see fit.

And your Petitioner shall ever pray &c..

The mark of Jane Smith, daughter of the said X The mark of Sarah Callaway, Sister X
Rebecca Smith

The mark of Wm Prior, Brother   of William Callaway, her Husband
of Sarah Prior, his wife X   of Rebecca Flower, Sister in law
of Mary Newman, Sister   of Eliza Flower, Sister in law
of Jemima Holloway, Sister in law

Appeal for clemency from family: This heartfelt appeal for Rebecca's life was signed by her family but was refused by Home Secretary Sir George Grey.

Your petitioners most earnestly implore Your Majesty, that the sentence of death passed on the said Rebecca Smith, may be commuted to such other punishment as your Majesty in your wisdom and mercy may see fit.

And your petitioners shall ever pray

The mark of Jane Smith, daughter of the said Rebecca Smith
The signature of William Prior, brother
The mark of Sarah Prior, his wife
The mark of Mary Newman, sister
The mark of Sarah Callaway, sister
The mark of William Callaway, her husband
The mark of Rebecca Flower, sister in law
The mark of Eliza Flower, sister in law
The mark of Jemima Holloway, sister in law

The missive was sent by Lambeth lawyer Henry Francis, who attached a letter addressed to The Right Honourable Sir George Grey, saying 'on behalf of the friends of Rebecca Smith now under sentence of death in Devizes Gaol, I am instructed to ascertain from you whether the recommendation of the jury in her favour will be taken into consideration.

Notably, Phillip Smith is not among the nine family members who signed the heartfelt plea for mercy. The list was topped by her 17-year-old daughter Jane, and Sarah Callaway – the sister who had been sadly compelled to give evidence against Rebecca at her trial. Her husband William Callaway, her sister Mary Newman, brother William Prior and three sisters in law were also named on the petition. All bar William made their mark – he signed his name in full. Rebecca's other sister Elizabeth Taylor had died suddenly eight months before as she carried water from the well in Bratton.

But the heartfelt plea was destined to fail. Judge Cresswell who had presided at the trial, worn the deadly black cap, and who had warned Rebecca not to expect clemency, made what can only be a pre-emptive strike, penning a letter of explanation to the Home Secretary. In the letter, he said he never had any doubt as to the verdict and added that Rebecca had confessed in full following the court case. He enclosed a copy of his notes of the evidence – 'in order that Sir George Grey may have all the information which is in my power to give him.'

Letter sent on behalf of Sir George Grey to Henry Francis rejecting his appeal for clemency.

Just days later, Sir George wrote letters to the petitioners in which he said he regretted he could find 'no grounds on which to justify in interfering with the course of law'. The letter, sealing Rebecca's fate, was received on August 20. She had just days to live. Twenty years later, when giving evidence to the Royal Commission on capital punishment, Sir George referred to Rebecca's case, stressing there had been no chance of commuting the sentence due to the evidence of pre-planning and of deliberate poisoning.

Rebecca remained in custody awaiting her death. We also know that the day before she died, she was visited by her sister, brother, and her husband Phillip. We do not know what he said to her, but his behaviour was so unfeeling that it warranted comment from the prison officers. Her relatives were overcome with weeping. Her surviving daughter Jane remained at home ill.

We know her last night was restless, but on waking she recovered her calm and ate a moderate breakfast. From 9am that morning the chaplain the Reverend Alexander Manning, who had been with her until late the night before, was with her again.

The prison had special rules about prisoners condemned to death – the chaplain was to visit daily. However, Rev Manning is said to have visited Rebecca 39 times during her 31 day stay at the prison. He was also with her constantly on the day of her execution. Looking at other reports of condemned prisoners it is likely that the chaplain not only urged Rebecca to confess but also to prepare for death.

From the first day of imprisonment she was said to be weighed down and oppressed by her crime and paid great attention to the chaplain who was appointed to watch over and instruct her and prepare her to meet her God. Rebecca's conduct from the first to the last day of imprisonment was described as most becoming. The *Devizes and Wiltshire Gazette* noted: 'Mild and contented in her manner and deportment, it might be thought that she was totally incapable of the unnatural crime of which she was committed'.

It added that she was free from guile and hypocrisy, she acknowledged the justice of the fate that awaited her and frequently expressed hope that others would take a warning by her fate. The *Wiltshire Independent* stated that she died with

> a full conviction of the enormity of her guilt deeply and painfully impressed upon her, and that she was sustained by a humble hope that, great as was her crime, her Saviour would look upon her with mercy and intercede for her at the Throne of Grace'. She was described as of a kind disposition, 'and anything but that callous, hardened wretch from which such a crime might have been expected.

As the day of her hanging approached, so did the excitement and anticipation of the many who would come to see her end. Rebecca's hanging proved a macabre attraction. Many would have come into town on Thursday anyway as it was market day, but the usual crowd was swollen by sightseers. Outside the prison the roads coming into Devizes were thronged with thousands of people coming in to witness the hanging on foot, on horseback, in carriages and carts. All the roads were packed, but those from Westbury, Bradford and Trowbridge were especially busy.

There appears sadly to have been a carnival-type atmosphere. The *Wiltshire Independent* newspaper writes of mothers with babes in arms and little children held by their hands. Carriages, carts and all sorts of other conveyances jammed the roads. The canal which ran alongside the prison and afforded a view was also packed with boats and we know that among them was a pleasure boat from Pewsey wharf decked out in evergreens and put on just for this occasion.

There were many more women than men and it was not just poorer people. There were women dressed in silks with parasols to protect their complexion against the August sun. It was estimated that between thirty and forty thousand people came to view the hanging, and the *Wiltshire*

Independent stated that such a multitude of people had never been seen in Devizes before. It commented too on the atmosphere saying:

'The usual levity of conduct, much of a piece, but worse than that which is generally witnessed at pleasure fairs of a low order, was prevalent. In short, the scene below the gallows was as disgusting, as that on it was soul sickening'. By the time the execution took place there was not a space to be had in the fields, roads and walls around the prison and it was said that Devizes marketplace was eerily silent and filled with the empty carriages and carts that had ferried the sightseers. At 11 o clock, the county's Under Sheriff arrived with a large posse of javelin men in their livery. The hangman, 49-year-old Thomas Calcraft, had stayed the previous night at the prison, as was his custom prior to an execution.

Devizes Market Place: The day of Rebecca's death was also market day in Devizes but the marketplace was deserted as thousands flocked to see her hang.

Calcraft was the official executioner for the city of London and travelled all over the country for his gruesome occupation. In his career, he carried out 450 executions, of whom 35 were women. He was sadly a celebrity in his own right – often playing to the crowd at public executions.

Calcraft's story is worth recounting and was the subject of a biography and several broadsides and chapbooks. Born at Chelmsford in 1800, he came to London when a boy. At 25 he married and reportedly was a devoted and loving husband and father – 'his wedded life was one of unclouded sunshine' according to *The Life and Recollections of Calcraft The Hangman*. However, given that this bestseller was penned relying on numerous interviews with Calcraft, we may have to take its contents with a large pinch of salt! There was also an account of his life called *The Groans of the Gallows*. This was printed in 1847 as what was known as a chapbook – a small affordable booklet that had all the pages printed on one sheet and then cut and folded to shape. The British Library still has a copy of this book which would have been sold at hangings and which paints an ugly picture of Calcraft's manners and practices.

His road to the unusual career of hangman started when he was selling pies to the crowds attending the execution of James Hunton in London in December 1828. He fell into conversation with the hangman John Foxton, and later, on his recommendation, was employed to flog offenders at Newgate prison.

When Foxton died, Calcraft successfully applied for the post of hangman and was sworn in as public executioner at the council chamber of the Guildhall. The ritual of the swearing in was solemn – judges sat at a high bench above which was a scroll saying 'Whoso sheddeth man's blood by man also shall his blood be shed'.

Calcraft, described as a short thickset man, slightly pockmarked, with large mouth, rather thick lips, and very thick short black curly hair, was dressed in his best suit and wore a high collared coat. As part of the ceremony he was required to take an oath with one hand on the executioner's axe and the other on the Bible. His first execution took place a week later. This was of Esther Hibner, who had been convicted of the death of a young girl, one of several which she had taken from London workhouses, ostensibly to teach them a trade. Instead the young girls were starved, beaten, and made to work from three in the morning.

Esther Hibner refused to walk or stand and had to be carried in a straitjacket to the scaffold. She constantly complained she had not had a fair trial. 'Jack Ketch shall never lay hands on me' she told officers as they came to take her to the scaffold. At this time, Jack Ketch was a byword for an executioner. Ketch was the infamous executioner at the time of Charles II and James II and was renowned for his barbarity and botched executions, the most famous and gruesome of which was of the Duke of

Monmouth at which he took five chops to behead the victim, incensing the crowd which threatened to tear him to pieces.

Calcraft himself also gained a gruesome reputation for favouring what was known as the short drop in hanging his victims. In a short drop, depending on the weight of the victim, many were more likely to die of strangulation and there are frequent reports of Calcraft hangings where victims struggled for several minutes before they died. Some even managed to scramble back up onto the scaffold. In 1856 for instance, Calcraft was the hangman for Soho murderer William Bousfield at Newgate. Described as a very tall man, he managed to get his feet on the drop and tried to free himself from the noose. Calcraft pushed him off, only for the victim to get his legs back up onto the platform. Calcraft pushed him off for a third time and, from under the drop, seized hold of the man's legs and swung on them.

Calcraft's reputation even led to him receiving death threats, but he frequently played to the crowds by swinging from the legs of his unfortunate victims. He also found ways of supplementing his income by selling the clothes of the victims, sometimes to Madame Tussauds, and even selling sections of the rope used to hang his victims, for which he charged between five shillings and £1 per inch. He did not always get the full financial benefit though – there are reports of tricksters in the crowds selling bits of old rope that they professed to be of the execution.

Another occasion when Calcraft fell foul of the crowd was at the hanging of John Holloway, convicted of murdering his wife, Celia. There was an old superstition that stroking by the hand of a hanged man could cure a multitude of illnesses. One man who had a large unsightly wen, or growth, on his neck, had arranged with Calcraft, doubtless for a fee, to try out this bizarre treatment. Once Holloway was dead, Calcraft untied his arms and, taking hold of one of the dead man's hands, proceeded to stroke the wen on the man's neck.

The crowd began to hiss, hoot and yell, and Calcraft was reprimanded by the sheriffs who reminded him his job was to kill not cure! From the eighteenth century through to when public hangings ended in 1868, the touch of a freshly hanged man's hand (it had to be male rather than female) was often sought after to cure swellings or lesions. The hangman could be bribed to effect this unusual cure. In Thomas Hardy's short story, 'The Withered Arm', Gertrude is advised by Conjuror Trendle to have the said arm stroked at the next hanging.

CALCRAFT'S FIRST INTERVIEW WITH THE EXECUTIONER.

Hangman Thomas Calcraft: Thomas Calcraft was the executioner at Rebecca's hanging. He was the official executioner for the city of London and sadly a celebrity in his own right – often playing to the crowd at public executions.

There was, in fact, a whole raft of superstitions around hanging and the gallows itself. A piece of wood taken from the gallows was used as a cure for ague or toothache. It would be worn in a bag around the neck. For toothache, the wood was rubbed on the tooth or the gum.

The hangman's rope was believed to have special powers – a strand of it wound round the neck was said to cure epilepsy, headaches, ague and bad eyes. It was even mentioned as far back as the first century AD, with Pliny mentioning it in his *Natural History* (AD 77). Some people believed the hangman's rope could not only effect cures but could bring great worldly prosperity. These bizarre relics were especially treasured by cardplayers as a guarantee for success.

Thankfully Calcraft had no recourse to any of his gruesome crowd-pleasing antics when he carried out Rebecca's execution. When the time came for her hanging, Calcraft, the county assistant sheriff and the chaplain went to her cell where Calcraft bound her hands and later wrapped ropes around her skirts for decency. The chaplain accompanied

THE EXECUTION of REBECCA SMITH AT DEVIZES 1849

Contemporary painting of Rebecca Smith's hanging.

her to the scaffold, reciting the burial service as they went.

Rebecca seemed composed and her step was firm. Once the rope was round her neck, Calcraft placed a hood over her head, she raised her hands in prayer, and died quietly without a struggle or a word.

The crowd were quiet, decent, and orderly as the execution took place but quickly regained their ghastly carnival atmosphere as they walked back to town. We have an idea of how many people there must have been because it was said to have taken an hour before the site was cleared.

The marketplace was quickly filled and was reported to being like a fair, with shows, music, and ballad singers. It was an opportune day for crime too. Pickpocket Stephen Powers, 14, took advantage of the crowds returning in New Park Street and filched the purse of Sarah Croker. The purse contained £4. He was sentenced to three months in prison and two whippings.

He was a member of another gang which had attended the execution with the intent of stealing. These two men and two women were found guilty of stealing a purse containing £15 from a Mrs Taylor of Dilton Marsh. She had come into town to see the execution and had adjourned with a friend to the Oddfellows Arms where the theft took place.

When the case was heard at the Devizes borough sessions, the gang were found guilty, and sentenced to prison with one habitual offender being transported. However, Mrs Taylor and her friend came in for a tongue lashing from the Recorder who was presiding and expressed his reluctance to award prosecution expenses to them. He deplored the fact that they had come to see Rebecca's execution, saying:

> It is truly lamentable that persons in a decent condition of life like yourselves should have derived gratification, and have come such a number of miles as you appear to have travelled, to see the agony and death of one of your fellow creatures, and that one of your own sex.

Unfortunately, the newspaper report does not record any response from the two women!

Expenses for Rebecca's execution came to £22 and sixteen shillings. Of this, £12 and ten shillings was paid to Calcraft. Rebecca was buried in the grounds of Devizes prison, escaping the fate of medical dissection that was the grisly end of many who were hanged for murder. It was the practice for criminals to be buried in unconsecrated ground and then to be covered in quicklime. When the prison was demolished in 1930, the burial ground was dug up and the remains sent to the Home Office. It filled only an envelope.

Coverage of Rebecca's trial and of her hanging appeared in newspapers all over England, Scotland, Ireland and Wales. Publications from the *Morayshire Advertiser* through to the *North Devon Journal*, from the *Express* in London to the *Dublin Evening Mail*, covered her plight. There were even reports in the *Lady's Newspaper*, a publication launched in 1847 and one of the very first aimed exclusively at a female readership.

While reports were likely filed, and often attributed to, the first-hand accounts published in local newspapers like the *Devizes Gazette* and the *Wiltshire Independent*, many publications put their own slant on the news, often in editorial or comment pieces.

The *Aberdeen Herald* for instance even suggested, hopefully ironically, that Rebecca had 'evidently adopted a practical philosophy of the Malthusian School'. Thomas Malthus was a celebrated economist whose treatise on population growth, published in 1798, would have been well known to the paper's audience. He had written 'the increase in population is necessarily limited by the means of subsistence.

Other newspapers added salacious details of their own – more than one telling its readers that Rebecca had applied arsenic to her breasts and suckled her babies to kill them. Some reported as if it were fact, that Rebecca had murdered all her children.

But not all were so radical in condemning Rebecca. The *Wiltshire Independent* for instance ran several letters opposing the concept of capital punishment. And on the very same page that it reported her execution, its editorial raised not only the question of capital punishment *per se*, but pinpointed ways in which such crimes as Rebecca's might be avoided. It criticised the ease at which poison could be purchased and urged the government to impose stricter rules. It also suggested there should be more attention paid to the issuing of death certificates – saying that the current law was 'very loose and deficient'. And it concluded by offering mitigation for Rebecca saying

> The want of all ordinary motive would seem to imply a morbid state of mind, which, if it can be ever urged as a plea for the mitigation of capital punishment, might be urged on behalf of the wretched Rebecca Smith.

Let us end this examination of Rebecca's sorry end on a personal note. When I was first told her story, more than 30 years ago, it was from a local Bratton historian Jean Morrison who in turn had heard it from an old lady who had been told it by her grandmother – a wonderful example of oral history in action. But one aspect of the story does not ring true – Mrs Morrison had been assured the sky went dark when Rebecca was hanged. I can find no reference to that in any newspaper report, so have to conclude that it did not happen – journalists would not have missed such a detail!

9

THE AFTERMATH

THERE WERE many changes in the years following Rebecca's death – changes to the law, to public attitudes, to public hanging and to the sale of poisons like arsenic. Rebecca Smith was the last woman ever to be hanged in Britain for infanticide of her own child. While many others came after her with similar sad stories, they were all either acquitted or given a lesser sentence. Over time the attitude towards infanticide began to change, with judge and jury giving more consideration to mental health and to extenuating circumstances.

But this all came too late for Rebecca. Home Secretary Sir George Grey was responsible for refusing the pleas for mitigation of her sentence. Had he agreed, Rebecca might have faced transportation instead of ending her life on the scaffold at Devizes. However, discussing the case in the 1870s as part of the review into capital punishment, Lord Grey said it had been impossible to give any sentence but that of death as the evidence had shown so very clearly that Rebecca had planned the murder of her baby.

Following Rebecca's tragic end, many women continued to appear in court on charges of infanticide, but their defence was that the act had been spontaneous, unplanned, and borne of mental illness, shock or distressing circumstances. Rebecca's confession of deliberate poisoning of her babies for fear they would come to want, did not fit the profile for mercy.

Newspapers continued to report sad instances of young single women giving birth alone and hiding the stillborn baby, or of others who tried drowning themselves and their child through hardship and distress. But increasingly their tragic cases were judged with compassion and understanding.

In Warminster in 1895 for instance, domestic servant Harriet Hopkins gave birth in secret and murdered her baby with a billhook, incurring no less than 23 injuries. But when she appeared before the court, the doctor who attended her after the birth suggested she had been suffering from puerperal delirium. The jury found her guilty of murder but agreed she was insane at the time.

Just nine years after Rebecca's trial, new mother Agnes Bradley was acquitted of killing her baby, with the jury acquitting her on grounds of insanity. The court had been told she had become insane after the birth and had killed her baby by mixing laudanum into the food. The judge at the trial was said to be so affected by the case that he shed tears in the court.

And when in 1887, 22-year-old Emily Spencer faced a charge of attempted infanticide for trying to drown herself and her baby at Enford near Pewsey, the trial was adjourned to allow for an inquiry into her mental health.

But infanticide did continue to be of national concern in Victorian England and opinion continued to be divided. Newspaper columns featured opinions and debate, with suggestions ranging from setting up foundling hospitals where single women could leave their babies, through to the prosecution of the fathers of illegitimate offspring.

A front-page editorial in the *Pall Mall Gazette* in 1865 considered the prevalence of infanticide saying

> There is scarcely a village in England in which girls cannot be pointed out who have incurred, more or less strongly, the suspicion of infanticide. One has had three children, who died in infancy about the same age; another had one killed by a fall; another by an overdose of some pernicious medicine; another found her baby suffocated in bed one morning.

Reporting on the trial of baby farmer and murderer Charlotte Winsor in 1865, the *Leeds Mercury* commented 'the extent to which infanticide prevails is appalling'. It went on to examine the subject concluding 'It is the old story of man's perfidy and woman's frailty'.

At a meeting of the British Association in 1865, a motion was discussed that would allow illegitimate children to be admitted to workhouses without their mother – a suggestion that purported to prevent infanticide. And when in 1863 the Society for the Prevention of Infanticide was formed, the *London Review* opined that it was not a day too soon saying 'The evil has indeed reached alarming proportions'.

And some critics were becoming concerned that juries were unwilling to convict women who killed their own children, saying that 'sentimental considerations have covered the blackness of the crime'.

In looking at the clamour and concerns over infanticide, it is necessary to place this within the context of the Victorian age when the role of women was epitomised by motherhood. Queen Victoria, mother of nine children, was upheld as a shining beacon of motherhood and marriage, and motherhood was considered the ultimate role and fulfilment for women. Rejection of this role, particularly in dreadful circumstances, was considered abhorrent.

Of course, infanticide was nothing new. Its sad history stretches right back to primeval times, and it has always been a part of human society. In ancient Europe and Asia, babies were abandoned and left to die from exposure as a means of controlling family numbers and economy.

Greek myths are full of instances of babies being exposed to die, and indeed Aristotle even advocated that in the case of congenital deformity, a child should not be allowed to live. One enduring myth even sees the purported founders of Rome, Romulus and Remus, being raised by a wolf after being exposed to die. Christianity, Judaism and Islam beliefs have always condemned infanticide with the Qur'an stating, 'You shall not kill your children for fear of want'.

However, in patriarchal societies such as in some parts of India, gender selective infanticide – female infanticide or abortion of female babies – continues. Male children are considered more desirable with men being more employable, earning higher wages and supporting the family's social and economic stability. In the tradition of extended families, sons were relied upon to provide for parents while a daughter would inevitably leave to join her new family when she married.

So what changed? In 1922 the Infanticide Act effectively abolished the death penalty for a woman who killed her new-born child while the balance of her mind was disturbed – it was a forerunner of the partial murder defence of diminished responsibility that did not become legal until 1957.

Attitudes were changing fast in all sorts of ways in Victorian England. One significant change following Rebecca's death was the abolition of public hangings. The grisly public exhibitions, which had attracted thousands and earned the reprobation of many, finally ended in 1868. The last public execution took place at Newgate on 26 May 1868 just three days before the law changed to end public hanging. Fenian

Michael Barrett was hanged by Calcraft. Barrett had been sentenced to death for his part in the 1867 Clerkenwell Outrage, when attempts to free a prisoner by using a barrel of gunpowder concealed in a costermonger's barrow damaged several houses and resulted in the deaths of 12 people.

The Capital Punishment Amendment Act received Royal assent on 29 May 1868. It said that all prisoners sentenced to death should be executed within the walls of the prison and formalised that procedure such as the holding of a coroner's inquest within 24 hours of the execution, and the presence of a prison surgeon to certify death. It also laid down who should attend the execution. This included the prison chaplain, the prison governor, the surgeon and the sheriff. Relatives of the condemned prisoner were also able to attend provided it was agreed by the sheriff and the prison's visiting justices.

Abolition of public hanging had been one of the recommendations of the Royal Commission on Capital Punishment 1864-66. There had also been considerable campaigning to end the practice, with Sir Robert Peel and Charles Dickens among many who called for the end to public hanging. On 16 December 1969, under Prime Minister Harold Wilson, MPs voted to abolish the death penalty for murder. The voting was 343 in favour and 185 against with all three party leaders, Harold Wilson, Jeremy Thorpe and Edward Heath, voting for abolition. It was passed by the House of Lords two days later with a majority of 46.

And what of Calcraft, the infamous executioner who ended Rebecca's life? By the time he was forced to retire in 1874, he had carried out 450 executions, 35 of which were of women. One of his later executions was at the age of 69, when *The Times* newspaper condemned his work saying: 'the adjustment of the rope was slow and bungling and such as to show that Calcraft's age has unfitted him for his occupation'. He died in December 1879 and left behind a reputation for his inhumane methods like the grisly short drop, which meant he had often to climb on the shoulders or pull on the legs of victims to end their lives.

There were changes too regarding the sale of deadly poisons. We have already seen how absurdly easy it had been for Rebecca to obtain arsenic. But in 1851, just two years after her death, the government introduced The Sale of Arsenic Regulation Act. This tightened the often-lax regulations around the sale of the deadly compound. It required sellers to have a written record of the purchaser, complete with name, address, occupation, and reason for the proposed use of the arsenic. The buyer also had to sign the register. Incidences of poisoning by arsenic declined for another reason too. Scientific advances meant that death by arsenic could be detected more readily and accurately even after a body had been buried for years. One of the pioneers in this was William Herapath, the Bristol professor who had given the evidence that secured Rebecca's conviction.

But what of Rebecca's family, left behind after this tragedy? The last record of husband Phillip refers to his bad behaviour when he saw Rebecca in prison. We know that his furniture was seized to pay rent and taxes but apart from this, there is no trace – no entries on a census, no references in the death records, no mentions in the criminal records. Perhaps he changed his name?

We know Rebecca's sisters Sarah Callaway and Mary Newman remained living in Bratton. In the 1851 census Sarah and her family are listed with her husband William being noted as a farmer of 15 acres employing one labourer. Sarah had been six years old when Rebecca was born. She married William Callaway on November 4, 1819 at Bratton church, raised six children, and died in 1864.

Mary, born four years after Rebecca in 1811, had married farm labourer Joseph Newman and raised four children. She died in 1884 aged 73.

Elizabeth, Rebecca's third sister, who had been born one year before her in 1806, had died just months before Rebecca was hanged. The mother of two sons died suddenly on Boxing Day 1848, while carrying water from a well to her home in Bratton. Her death was recorded in the Baptist chapel minutes. Her widower, William Taylor, and her two sons Edward and William, moved to Westbury and by 1851 they were living in Alfred Street.

The house where Rebecca started her troubled marital life no longer exists. The Elizabethan farmhouse, known as Whites, had once belonged to the Whitaker family but had been sold and subdivided into cottages for farm workers. It was destroyed by the War Department in 1952 after it purchased the farm in order to add to its lands on the Imber ranges. Today the site is occupied by new houses.

But what of Jane, Rebecca's surviving daughter? Her sad plight had been brought to the attention of *Economist* founder and Westbury MP James Wilson, who in turn asked fellow Liberal MP George Cornewall Lewis for help and advice. Lewis had been a poor law commissioner and was now Under Secretary of State for Home Affairs.

James Wilson's letter describes Phillip Smith as a 'sad reprobate' but also gives a rare description of 18-year-old Jane, describing her as young, innocent, delicate and genteel looking 'far beyond what one could expect'. Since her mother's death and the loss of her family home she had been living with a poor respectable neighbour, but local people were keen that she should be sent away to make a living where her tragic history was not known.

His comments also reveal something of local attitudes towards her and her shocking history, saying 'the people round here where she was known have a natural aversion to take her into their service. Is there any establishment that you know of where she could be placed to learn household work and from which she might afterwards procure a place?'

Jane, who had experienced the deaths of her ten siblings and who had made her mark on the family's unsuccessful appeal for clemency for her condemned mother, left Wiltshire, left England, left her life, for a new start on the other side of the world. She emigrated to Australia, leaving England never to return. The first reference to her departure comes in the minutes of the Westbury and Whorwellsdown workhouse of February 1 1850 which states: 'Resolved that the sum of £3 be advanced towards the expenses of the emigration of Jane Smith belonging to this parish to Australia subject to the approval of the Poor Law Board.'

Interestingly this is signed by the chairman of the board of guardians, Joshua Whitaker. This is the same Joshua Whitaker who had

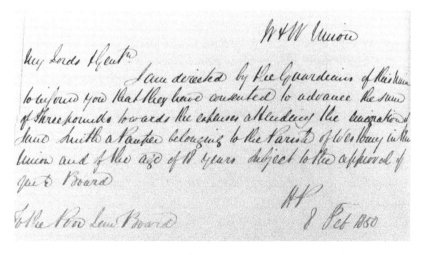

Jane's emigration costs: This excerpt from the logbooks of the Board of Guardians of the Westbury and Whorwellsdown workhouse notes their agreement to fund part of the emigration costs for Jane Smith, described as a pauper of the parish

been executor for the wills of Rebecca's parents and who lived near the Prior family in Bratton. He must have known of Jane and her plight.

Later minutes record that the request was approved. On March 15 1850 it was noted that three pounds had been paid to Thomas Pearce for the emigration costs of Jane Smith.

Jane would have been supplied with an outfit and extra clothing and at least £1 for bedding money. The workhouse guardians paid her fare to the port where she embarked as well as paying for part of her passage.

Jane was not the first to be helped through the workhouse – though it is unlikely she was ever a resident there. The Poor Law Amendment Act of 1834 had stipulated that provision could be made for the emigration of the poor with the cost being borne by the emigrant's home parish. In 1850, the Westbury workhouse had been full to overflowing, with the guardians even taking on extra staff to cope with them. Doubtless emigration was an attractive alternative to a life of penury.

Emigration to Australia, Canada and America had first become popular in the 1830s and 1840s and reached a peak in the 1850s. Most people were driven to take their chances in a faraway country simply through need and desperation. High unemployment, low wages, few prospects and the Irish potato famine led to thousands of people leaving their homes. Australia alone saw 58,000 immigrants in just 25 years. Newspaper columns in Britain were packed with letters from people who had settled there, boasting about the good life, the cheap food, the high wages and the opportunity to become landowners.

A letter from a James Mead printed in the *Salisbury and Winchester Journal* in March 1849 begs his family to join him in Australia saying, 'there is more good beef given to the dogs at this one station in one week than is eaten by the whole of the people in your parish in twelve months'.

And on the very same page where the *Wiltshire Independent* reported the inquest into baby Richard's death, a lengthy letter was printed from another emigrant painting a rosy picture of his new life, saying:

> Who would stop in Old England and starve when they can come over here and make their fortune in ten years…do not hesitate one day, but go and get your papers, and come out here to the Land of Paradise'.

The writer ended with handy tips for would be emigrants, such as remembering to line clothes trunks with tin before the journey.

In newspapers nationwide there were advertisements for *The Emigrants' Almanack*, for sale at just threepence, and covering every detail from conduct on board ship and tips for treatment of sea sickness

Jane's emigration: Rebecca's daughter Jane was among many women leaving to make a new life away from England. She sailed on board the Lloyds ship, arriving in Australia in June 1850 (see also next page).

through to the prices of provisions and rates of postage – invaluable in enabling the emigrants to keep in touch with the relatives left behind.

Societies aimed at promoting emigration were formed throughout the country including Wiltshire, and an Emigration Fund was even set up specifically to promote female emigration – with the Queen and Prince Albert contributing £500.

Australia was a particularly attractive proposition for young single women, who were actively encouraged to emigrate to solve the gender imbalance of areas like New South Wales, which had only ceased to be a penal colony in 1840. England had been sending convicts there since 1788

Single young women had to satisfy certain conditions to emigrate – they had to be of good character and health, able to read and write, and preferably have a skill.

Jane's emigration records are fascinating. They list her age as 18, that she can read and write and that she is a needlewoman. Her home village is noted as Bratton (misspelt Britton) and her parents, Rebecca and Phillip are noted as 'both dead'. It is impossible to know whether Phillip really was dead at this time but as emigration of a young single woman required the permission of parents, it was probably convenient for Jane to say he was. The form also states that Jane was in good health and had no complaints during her voyage.

She travelled on a ship called Lloyds which was no stranger to the journey to Australia having made the voyage at least ten times. The Lloyds was a three masted wooden barque of 403 tons built in London in 1830. It had been a convict ship. In 1833 and 1837 it sailed to New South Wales carrying 200 convicts on each voyage. Convicts on board had been sentenced to an average of nine years, though several faced life sentences. In July 1845, the Lloyds sailed to Van Diemen's Land with 170 passengers – only two among them had life sentences. Van Diemen's Land (Tasmania) had been used as a convict colony after New South Wales.

The Lloyds had also been used to carry emigrants to New Zealand in 1841 when 67 children under the age of 14 died due to an outbreak of whooping cough on board.

Jane started her journey in Plymouth where she may have been housed in one of the many specialist lodgings set up especially for female single emigrants. On board, young single women would have been supervised and given tasks such as needlework. There was also basic education on the 100-day voyage. Her sleeping quarters would have been with fellow young women. The lower deck was divided into three sections, single women at the prow, married couples in the middle, and single men at the stern.

On Jane's voyage, she was one of 191 passengers excluding the captain and crew. There were 74 men and 69 women – 52 of the women were single. There were also 48 children including four babies under the age of one. Fortunately, there were no deaths during the voyage. Many of the emigrants came from Ireland and had worked in agriculture with occupations listed on the ship's register including shepherds, carters, farmers and labourers.

The Lloyds arrived at Port Phillip in New South Wales on 29 June 1850. Jane, like other single women, would have been received and lodged in a female only reception area from where she would have been helped to get a job and accommodation.

It is difficult to trace Jane after her arrival but it appears that she stayed in Australia, living in the Merendee and Mudgee areas, about 160 miles northwest of Port Phillip. It was a gold mining area where gold was discovered in the 1850s, sparking a stampede of prospectors and a massive increase in population. Sydney went from a population of 39,000 in 1850 to 200,000 in just 20 years.

Jane died on 25 January 1908, having been married twice and given birth to six children. She died as Jane Canning and is buried in Merendee cemetery in New South Wales.

PERSONAL FOOTNOTES

I FIRST heard about Rebecca Smith when I was a first-time mother living in Bratton in the 1980s. I was told her tale by local historian Jean Morrison – a remarkable woman who was a scholar, historian, folklorist and a fount of local knowledge. Much of her vast collection of artefacts including her historic costumes is now in Trowbridge Museum while her research and writings can be seen at the Wiltshire and Swindon History Centre and in Devizes Museum.

Mrs Morrison had personally heard the story of Rebecca Smith in the 1970s from a very old woman in the village who in turn had heard it from her grandmother – so this really was oral history in action. The old lady even told Mrs Morrison that the sky had turned dark at the very moment Rebecca died.

Researching someone whose unhappy fame came at the end of her life and in unfortunate circumstances is by its very nature difficult. Unpicking the lives of ordinary working people has always been challenging – not for nothing is it said that history is written by the rich and the victors.

Such people, often barely literate, do not leave journals or written records, often do not have gravestones marking their death and will not be mentioned in newspapers unless, like Rebecca, they fall foul of the law. There is no mention of Rebecca in Marjorie Reeves's wonderful *Sheep Bell and Ploughshare* which traces the history of Bratton life and families, though it must surely have been the talk of the village. Neither is her demise mentioned in the minutes of the Bratton Baptist chapel where she and her family were regular worshippers. There are no gravestones marking her ten babies.

And yet her sad story would have reached people throughout the country and may have helped to throw a light on the plight of the disempowered and vulnerable Victorian woman.

Primary sources used range from censuses, births deaths and

marriage records, wills, newspaper reports, tithe maps and terriers, and the statistics of crime for 1849. I have also examined minute books of the Bratton Baptist chapel, the Westbury Leigh chapel and the West End formerly Cooks Stile chapel. I have looked at plans of the chapel graveyard and the minutes of the Board of Guardians at the Westbury and Whorwellsdown workhouse.

Newspapers used many column inches reporting on Rebecca's trial and execution, and these too were useful. Also too were the letters to the newspapers along with the editorials and opinion pieces that raised questions about everything from capital punishment to the ease with which arsenic could be obtained. They make fascinating reading.

Secondary sources include various articles that have appeared about Rebecca Smith, ranging from the sensational to the scholarly. There are many mentions of Rebecca in so-called murder anthologies but the very best article by far is that by Katherine Watson in her article on 'Religion, Community and the Infanticidal Mother'.

I also used source books about contraception, poisoning and the role of arsenic in Victorian Britain, the plight of agricultural labourers in Wiltshire and about Devizes prison and capital punishment.

Very special thanks go to archivist Steve Hobbs and the Wiltshire and Swindon History Centre and to Westbury Heritage Society and Wiltshire Museum Director David Dawson for the use of images.

When I started researching Rebecca's story, I lived in a cottage less than half a mile from the site of her home. My daughter was christened in the church where Rebecca married Phillip. Today, from my window in Westbury I can see the building where the inquest was held – the start of the journey that ended on the gallows.

REFERENCES

Chapter 1
Cobbett, W. (1830) *Rural Rides*
Wiltshire parish registers BMD *(Ancestry online)*
Census: Bratton, Westbury 1841/1851/1861 *(Ancestry online)*
Will of Sarah Pryor 15 November 1841 *Wiltshire and Swindon History Centre*
Will of William Pryor 28 January 1830 *WSHC*
Bratton Baptist Church minute book *WSHC*
Bratton Church Registers 1542-1812
Pugh R.B and Crittall Elizabeth *Victoria County History Volumes V and VIII*
Mclaren Angus *Birth Control in Nineteenth Century England: A Social and Intellectual History*
Doel, W. (1890) *Twenty Golden Candlesticks*
Pevsner N *The Buildings of England: Wiltshire*
Morrison J *Bratton's Worst Murder*: Wiltshire Folklife magazine
Reeves Marjorie *Sheep Bell and Ploughshare: The story of two village families*

Chapter 2
Cobbett, W. (1830) *Rural Rides*
Harris R and Colt Hoare R *The History of Modern Wiltshire: Hundred of Westbury*
Wiltshire County Archaeology Service: *The Archaeology of Wiltshire's Towns: An Extensive Urban Survey of Westbury*
Wiltshire parish registers BMD *(Ancestry online)*
Census: Westbury 1841/1851/1861 *(Ancestry online)*
The National Archives
Westbury and Whorwellsdown Union, Board of Guardians minute books 1835–1850 *WSHC*
Westbury and Whorwellsdown Union letter book 1848–1872 *WSHC*
British Newspaper Archive
Pigot's Directory of Wiltshire 1844 and 1822
Post Office Directory of Wiltshire 1855
Pugh R.B and Crittall Elizabeth *Victoria County History Volumes V and VIII*
Bates Stephen *Penny Loaves and Butter Cheap: Britain in 1846*
Parker D and Chandler J *Wiltshire Churches*
Roger K *Wiltshire and Somerset Woollen Mills*

Haynes R and Slocombe I *Wiltshire Toll Houses*
The History of Parliament *www.historyofparliamentonline.org*

Chapter 3
British Newspaper Archive
Sly N *Wiltshire Murders*
Notice for witnesses to appear at trial *WSHC*
Oxford Dictionary of National Biography
Bristol Civic Society *William Herapath*
The British Medical Journal *obituary of George Sylvester www.jstor.org*

Chapter 4
Watson Katherine *Poisoned Lives: English Poisoners and their Victims*
Wharton James C *The Arsenic Century*
Watson Katherine: *Religion, community and the infanticidal mother: evidence from 1840s rural Wiltshire*
British Newspaper archive: *www.bna.org.uk*

Chapter 5
Pugh R.B and Crittall Elizabeth: *Victoria County History Volume V*
Girven J: *Doing Time in Wiltshire*
Pigot's Directory: *www.specialcollections.le.ac.uk*
Buxton D: *Around Devizes in Old Photographs*
Pathe News: *Film of demolition of Devizes prison www.britishpathe.com*

Chapter 6
National Archives: *Criminal Register England and Wales 1791-1892, Indictment, account of trial, petition submitted by Rebecca Smith's family, petition submitted by John Fox, letters from Sir Cresswell Cresswell to H. Waddington (Home Secretary's office) Letter from Sir George Grey Home Secretary in response to petitions.*
British Newspaper Archive: *www.bna.org.uk*

Chapter 7
Wilson A *Forgotten Labour: The Wiltshire agricultural worker and his environs*
Married Women's Property Act 1882: *www.legislation.gov.uk*
Friedman S: *Mothers Who Kill, evolutionary underpinnings and infanticide law www.pubmed.ncbi.gov*
Watson K.D: *Religion, community and the infanticidal mother: evidence from 1840s rural Wiltshire*

Chapter 8
The Life and Recollections of Calcraft the Hangman

Dictionary of National Biography

British Library *The Groans of the Gallows – the past and present life of William Calcraft, the living hangman of Newgate (chapbook) www.bl.uk*

Chapter 9

Eyre and Spottiswood HMSO: *Report of the Capital Punishment Commission 1866*

1851 Sale of Arsenic Regulation Act *www.legislation.gov.uk*

1868 Capital Punishment Amendment Act *www.legislation.gov.uk*

1922 Infanticide Act *www.legislation.gov.uk*

1957 Homicide Act *www.legislation.gov.uk*

1965 Murder (Abolition of Death Penalty) Act *www.legislation.gov.uk*

Foundling Museum: *www.foundlingmuseum.org*

Barrington E: *Servant to All*, pp. 167-8

Census Westbury and Bratton 1851/1861/1871/1881

References to Emigration of Jane Smith: *www.nsw.org www.findagrave.com www.ancestry.co.uk*

Westbury and Whorwellsdown Union, Board of Guardians minute books 1835–1850 *WSHC*

Westbury and Whorwellsdown Union letter book 1848–1872 *WSHC*

INDEX

Lightning Source UK Ltd.
Milton Keynes UK
UKHW021300210822
407592UK00008B/383

9 781914 407345